D0912872

The Fundamentals
of
Sailboat Racing

The Fundamentals
of
Sailboat Racing

by

Stephen Ackley Falk

ST. MARTIN'S PRESS NEW YORK

Library of Congress Catalogue #73-79232
Manufactured in the United States of America
No part of this book may be reproduced without
permission in writing from the publisher.

St. Martin's Press
175 Fifth Avenue
New York, N.Y. 10010

AFFILIATED PUBLISHERS: Macmillan Limited, London
—also at Bombay, Calcutta, Madras and Melbourne

Table of Contents

Introduction

Rigging your boat for racing   10

Sailboat handling for speed in racing   14

Helmsmanship   32

Key racing situations   48

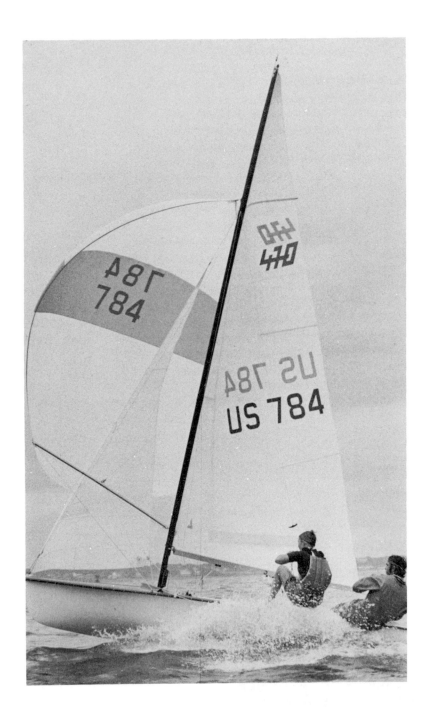

Introduction

There's nothing hard about winning a sailboat race. Just start well, sail a little bit faster than the others, and sail to the right places where wind, current, and competitors will give you the advantage. Get at least as much luck as the next fellow. And work at it!

This book is about how to do those things. It's a "how-to" book, long on practicality, low-keyed on theory except when it's really necessary. (Where more technical explanations are desirable, they've been tucked away in the back in the form of appendixes, where they are available for separate study rather than as interruptions to the basic reading.)

The illustrations and text emphasize the smaller classes of racing boats, since that's what most racers sail; however, if you sail in one of the larger keelboats or racing cruisers, you'll find that the same techniques apply.

This is a book for *sailboat racers*—skippers and crew. Whether just beginning in racing or reviewing many years of experience, you should find that it covers the complete range of things to do to race your boat, from pre-race preparation through helmsmanship techniques to mid-race strategy.

How Sailboats Race

Small sailboats race around "closed courses"—around marks, ending up pretty much where they start, as contrasted with ocean racers which normally race from place to place. The race committee designates a course for each race, which is varied to suit the direction and strength of the wind, by specifying a number of marks of the course and the side on which they are to be passed.

The race begins and ends on "lines" (often but not always the same line), which are bounded by two marks. One end of the line is a "committee boat," staffed by members of the race committee. Starting signals (and other signals) are made at the committee boat.

Starting is done by passing through the start line in the proper direction any time after the starting signal. A series of sight and sound signals are used to provide a countdown to the start "gun." One of the prime skill ingredients of racing is learning to "hit the line" at full speed immediately after the start signal. (If any part of the boat, crew, or equipment is over the line at the gun, the boat is a "premature starter" and must sail entirely back over the line and start again.)

Closed courses are almost always laid out so as to make the first leg of the course directly upwind, which helps to get the boats reasonably well spread apart before they arrive at the first turning mark.

The most common courses are triangular, providing a beat, a reach, and a run; often there is another beat to the finish. There is no single standard course; this is entirely a matter of judgment, left to the race committee.

(Note that a number of the courses, as illustrated, require moving the committee boat between the start and the finish; this is done so that their rule of "all marks to port"—or starboard—may include the mark which bounds one end of the start and finish lines.)

Sailing Racing Rules Summarized

Whenever two racing boats approach each other, one has right-of-way; the other is obligated to keep clear. Although the right-of-way boat is obliged to avoid unexpected maneuvers that might interfere with a boat attempting to keep clear, it is otherwise entitled to steer its proper course without interference or threat of collision. Any contact, or even near-collision that would require the right-of-way boat to alter course in order to avoid collision, would constitute a foul.

In case of a foul, the right-of-way boat should "protest," which should be announced by hailing "protest" or words to that effect then and there, and, except in singlehanded boats, a red flag or other locally approved protest flag is displayed. It is usually tied to a shroud.

Under the rules in effect beginning in 1973, the protest is obligatory in cases involving any contact between two boats—failing which any third boat may protest both boats involved in the contact.

The standard penalty for a boat found guilty of a foul is disqualification from the race—usually scored as last place plus one or two penalty positions. The rules, and good sportsmanship, require a skipper who knows he is guilty of a rule's infringement to withdraw immediately from the race. Most scoring systems provide a minor reward for such withdrawals, usually scoring the withdrawn boat as DNF (did not finish), the same number of points as last place. That's a point or two better than DSQ (disqualified).

Local race instructions, published for each regatta or race series, may allow lesser penalties. One of the most common is to permit the fouling boat, when it acknowledges the foul, to make a double turn in the water (720 degrees), after which the boat may continue racing without further penalty. Other systems may provide for demotion of the fouling boat, but for fewer positions than outright disqualification. Most such systems require that the fouling skipper immediately acknowledge the foul; if the matter has to go to a protest committee for "trial," disqualification for the skipper found guilty is the usual price.

The racing rules apply from the beginning of the race's timing sequence until after the boat has finished and sailed clear of the finish line. The rules apply to all racing boats, whether or not they are in the same race.

The following statements of the rules are very much simplified; for a complete understanding of the rules, most skippers will want to purchase and study a good textbook which contains the official text of the rules, as published by the North American Yacht Racing Union, together with explanatory text. One that we might recommend is *Sailing Racing Rules the Easy Way* by Falk (St. Martin's Press, Inc., New York, N. Y., 1973).

1. *Starboard tack boats have right-of-way over port tack boats.* Starboard tack means mainsail on the port side of the boat—boats running before the wind normally jibe onto starboard tack in order to get this right-of-way.

2. *Leeward boats have right-of-way over windward boats.* This rule applies only to boats that are on the same tack and overlapped—but it then decides the right-of-way in most

cases that weren't settled by "starboard tack."

3. *Overtaking boats keep clear.* Also a "same tack" rule, this does *not* mean that a starboard tacker has to look out when overtaking a port tacker. This rule often leads to trouble because too many beginners forget that overtaking ends when overlap begins. A boat that is passing (on the same tack) to leeward becomes a right-of-way leeward boat as soon as its foremost part overlaps the aftermost part of the overtaken boat.

4. *Buoy room must be given to boats overlapping on the inside.* The most complicated of the rules, this one leads to more fouls than any other. To be entitled to room, the boat claiming the inside overlap must either tack into the overlap, or establish the overlap by the time the nearer boat is within two lengths of the mark. If it is a "windward mark"—that is, tacking was required either to get to the mark or to round it—this rule applies only to boats on the same tack, and starboard tackers are not required to give buoy room to port tackers. If it is not a windward mark, this rule temporarily outweighs the "starboard tack" rule, and applies whether boats are on the same or different tacks. Remember, too, that when a boat does rate buoy room rights, that includes room for overlapping boats to tack or jibe whenever such a maneuver is normal to the course. A boat that is not overlapped does get the right to jibe close in front of others when turning the mark, but clear-ahead boats can tack only at their own risk. Buoy room rights do not count at starting marks.

5. *Obstructions require that inside boats be given room to pass safely.* Obstructions include other boats with right-of-way, and anything else large enough to require that you alter course significantly in order to pass safely. A boat that must tack to clear an obstruction can hail for room to do so. The obstruction rights rule applies whether or not boats are on the same tack, temporarily outweighing the "starboard tack" rule, *except before starting* (when starboard tack boats still have right-of-way over obstructed port tackers).

6. *All rights are forfeited when a boat is "returning."* Boats that were over the start line early have to return and restart, and while doing so have no rights over any other boat that is not also returning. Similarly, a boat that touches a mark (any touch, hull, lines, or crew counts) must return to re-

round that mark before she can continue the race—and she does so without any rights until after she has completed the re-rounding.

7. *Tacking and jibing boats keep clear of all others.* Between the time a tacking boat passes head-to-wind and the time she gets onto her new course, she must keep clear of boats on either tack. The same thing is true of a jibing boat between the time her mainsail crosses the centerline of the boat and the time it fills on the new tack. Either of these times is very short, but the important part of the rule comes into play when a boat gets a new right-of-way by tacking or jibing—the other boat is not required to anticipate that right-of-way, and is not obligated to begin keeping clear until the tack or jibe is completed; if it is then too late for her to keep clear, the tacking or jibing boat is guilty of a foul for making the maneuver too close.

8. *Leeward boats may luff windward boats.* Another complicated and often-misunderstood part of the rules, these rights are somewhat different before and after the start. Luffing means altering course toward the wind. *Before starting,* any overlapped leeward boat may luff (steer toward) a windward boat, but she must do so slowly, allowing the windward boat room and opportunity to keep clear. She may always steer at least as close to the wind as close-hauled; at any time that windward's helmsman is not forward of leeward's mast, leeward may luff further, up as far as head-to-wind. *After starting,* leeward may not luff above her proper course at all unless she has "luffing rights." If she does have luffing rights, she may luff hard, fast, and repeatedly. She gets luffing rights by being overtaken, or by having either of the boats tack or jibe ending up overlapped, or by converging into overlap from more than two lengths. Luffing rights end for the life of the overlap if ever the windward boat's helmsman gets "mast abeam"—that is, so the windward helmsman is even with, or forward of, leeward's mast. (Luffing applies only to same tack boats.)

I recommend the following memory-key for skippers first learning the rules: SLOBOAT.

S . . . *starboard* tack over port tack.
L . . . *leeward* boat over windward boat.
O . . . *overtaking,* keep clear.

B . . . *buoy room* for inside, overlapped boats.
O . . . *obstructions* rate room.
A . . . *all rights lost returning.*
T . . . *tacking and jibing,* keep clear.
and . . . luff 'em and leave 'em.

A final note: The racing rules are not entirely the same as the general rules-of-the-road. In the case of offshore races, the racing instructions usually direct that the rules-of-the-road will replace the racing rules after the boats have gotten to sea, or from dusk to dawn.

In brief, the rules-of-the-road give right-of-way to starboard tack boats over port tack boats, and to leeward boats when both are on the same tack.

If you are not certain that a nearby boat is racing, you should assume that it is not and follow the rules-of-the-road. When in doubt, why not hail and ask?

How to Get into Races

If you're really starting from scratch, the quickest way to learn to race is to serve as crew on someone else's boat. In that role, you'll have a chance to observe all of the procedures, and your skipper will be giving you full-time lessons from start to finish of every race . . . and most likely quite a bit before and after every race. If you already know the basics of sailing, you'll likely find that you learn all you need to know to skipper your own boat after half-a-dozen outings.

Getting a crewing job is the simplest thing in the world —most clubs have shortages of crews (because crews graduate so quickly to their own boats). Go to the nearest yacht club and post a simple notice on the bulletin board that says you'd like to crew with a skipper who'll teach you how to race, note your phone number and when you can be reached, and you're almost sure to be able to pick and choose your berth. If you're too impatient to wait for the phone to ring, go to the club an hour before their races start and stand around looking hopeful—chances are you'll get drafted by the second person you ask, "Know anyone who needs a crew?"

If you hanker for a crew's berth on an offshore racing boat, that takes a bit more planning. The bulletin board method may work as before, but you're probably best advised to work out some means of meeting with your potential skipper before you really go out with him for more than an afternoon's ride. If you can find an acquaintance who's a member of The Corinthians, ask him to tell you about how you can join the association—they provide a crew-reference service for their membership.

Increasing numbers of would-be crews take to the classified advertisements in sail-oriented magazines. Personally, I'd want to know who I'm sailing with before I go to sea for any period of time—and what kind of groceries they pack! Assuming that you have more offers than you need, feel free to talk things over with your potential skipper; make it clear that you want to learn—if he has no patience with beginners, you'll want to learn that before you leave the mooring. Also, don't neglect to discuss in detail what clothing and personal effects you'll need.

If you're ready to bypass the crewing role, and jump right into competition, all you need to do is get a boat and find a race.

Four considerations bear on deciding what kind of boat you should race in: price, complexity, physical demands of the boat, and availability of competition.

The smallest racing boats, such as Lasers, Sunfish, and a host of dinghies, cost under $1,000 ready to race. The next size (14 to 16 feet or so) such as 420's, 470's, Finns, runs $1,500 to $2,000 completely rigged. Another thousand in your budget could move you up to a Tempest, FD, or equivalent in the "hot" boat class. Between $3,000 and $5,000 will buy a very nice keel boat and get it decently equipped for racing—Soling, Ensign, etc., running up to 22 feet or so. Boats you can sleep on with reasonable comfort, and race in good company, tend to run 25 to 27 feet or more, and cost $10,000 to $15,000 with proper instruments and equipment.

A good secondhand boat, in racing condition, costs around 30 to 40 percent less than the new price.

Unless you're very familiar with the fine points of sailing and sail trimming, the sensible thing to do is to start racing in a simple boat. The fewer strings-and-things there are, the more you can concentrate on sailing the race. More and more of the better racing classes are placing tight restrictions on rigging modifications. For beginning racing, check into these kinds of class restrictions, and give preference to the boats that prohibit additions to rigging until you know enough about racing to compete with the innovators. Here's an easy rule of thumb—if you don't fully understand how to use all of the adjustments in a boat after two days in it, you're not ready to race it.

Pick a boat that you're physically able to handle in middling winds and seas. Unless you're very strong and athletic, the Finn or 505 isn't for you. Not that you may not be able to survive sailing it, but you simply won't be able to compete seriously with strong and agile opponents.

Once you've decided the price range and general kinds of boats you can handle, the key thing is to find out what classes are actively raced within your area. Think in terms of where it will be most convenient for you to do most of your racing, and then go see what they race there. Most likely, there will be a yacht club that's convenient for you, and if you're going to race at that club, well, you get the kind of boat they race.

There are some pretty "exclusive" yacht clubs, and you may not be able to gain membership immediately, so find out about that, of course, before you settle on a boat. The majority of clubs, however, are both reasonable in cost and easy about admittance, so don't be shy about going over and asking the club secretary about joining.

If there isn't a club that suits you nearby, there's still plenty of racing. Pick a boat you like, and write or call the class association to learn their racing schedule in your region.

Whatever kind of boat you're considering, they're bound to have a class association which not only controls design and manufacturing standards for the boat, but also sponsors and/or coordinates a full season of racing. Anyone who has a boat is welcome at any regatta the class schedules—simply show up at the right time and place, pay a registration fee (usually around $5, which goes toward trophies and maybe lunch), and get into the race.

The dealer you're considering buying the boat from will put you in touch with the class association and get you registered. If you want to check out more classes than are distributed in your town, look up the classes you like in the annual directories that are published by each of the better sailing magazines—or call the North American Yacht Racing Union (NAYRU) at 37 West 44th Street, New York City.

If you have one of the larger boats that can compete with others of similar size but different manufacture, what you do is get in touch with the Yacht Racing Association in your area. They'll give you a complete rundown on races in your kind of boat and how to get into them (either by joining a club that's active in that kind of racing, or by joining the regional association and showing up for races that are sponsored by members of the association). The nearest yacht club will tell you what and where the regional association is, or again you can call NAYRU.

Whether you join a yacht club, or race under the sponsorship of your class or regional association, you'll find that you and your boat are welcome at every regatta you can locate (except intraclub series racing and certain regattas for which there are published qualification requirements). So get the schedule, and get on the water. Practice goes a long way toward winning.

1

Rigging your boat for racing

There's no point in going out to race with a bucket tied to your stern—or with anything else that's going to slow you down. Obvious? Well then, it's just as important to be sure that you've done all the reasonable things to make sure that your boat is going to go as fast as it can. Mostly, setting your boat up right to race doesn't take any longer than doing it wrong—it only takes a little bit of knowing what's right.

The best way to find out how to set up your boat is to take a good look at how the better sailors in your area rig theirs. Since every class of boat has its own kind of strings-and-things, a detailed rigging plan could be right for only one class. We can give the basics, however, so that you'll know what to look for when you do look over the fleet champ's boat. (Ask him for the guided tour; my experience is that all of the top skippers are happy to comply with that flattering request—and you'll learn much more when he's along to point out what he does when rigging, and why.) Then look over the next best three or four skippers' boats, and find out what they do differently. You'll find that the truly important things will be done by most of the leaders in the same way. When there's big disagreement about how tight to rig this, or where to place that, it's likely to be unimportant.

Setting up sails and rigging

In setting up your sails, there are a limited number of things to adjust: halyard, clew outhaul, boom vang, gooseneck downhaul, and maybe a Cunningham. You may, if you sail a larger boat, have a backstay with adjustable tension, and maybe a separate adjustment to tighten the wire in the luff of your jib.

Even though the reasons are sometimes pretty complex, it turns out that *what* to do with these tension adjustments is very easy, and they all work on the same principle: *the harder the wind blows, the tighter she goes.* It's as simple as that: in light airs, don't set up tension more than almost-snug;

in middling winds, all adjustments are snug; in heavy airs, set them up taut.

Some boats have a "pressure batten" in the sail—a large, flexible batten that's a bit overlong for its pocket; you can then tie it into its pocket with or without tension. Tying the batten in tightly causes it to bend fairly sharply, helping shape the sail into a deeper curve.
This is the exception to the foregoing rule, for a pressure batten is tighter in light airs, and has less tension in heavier winds.

Appendix A reviews the usual settings of sails and standing rigging so you'll have a feel of what to look for when you get advice from experienced sailors in your class of boat.
Appendix B describes the special rigging techniques for lateen-rigged board boats including the Sunfish.
As you get more experience in setting up your sails, you'll want a really good explanation of how they're best shaped. I think the booklet *Sail & Air*, by sailmakers Charles Ulmer and John Stanton, provides an excellent grounding in sails and speed; with their permission, it is reproduced in Appendix C.

Cunningham rig for adjusting tension on mainsail luff; the line goes from hole (about a foot up from the tack) to a double-ended tackle; this in turn is led with one end to each side of the boat, where it can be reached for adjustment by skipper while on either tack. Increase tension in heavy winds, ease tension in lighter airs. (Also shown is the clew outhaul, led inside boom to block and jam cleat [underside of boom] where crew can adjust tension while sailing.)

Pre-Race Checkout

The silliest way to lose a race is to have a piece of gear come apart when it could easily have been checked.

Examine the boat *when you put it away,* in order to find anything that needs to be repaired or replaced before the next day's racing.

- Any worn-out lines? Halyards OK; sheets OK? Do you know what size and length (and material) is needed for replacements?
- Any loose cleats? Half a minute will check them all.
- Snaphooks and other fittings all OK? Springs still tight enough to hold? Another half-minute check.
- Other hardware items: turnbuckles all properly pinned? rudder fittings sound? centerboard hardware? gooseneck?
- Anything bent or worn? Look 'em over!
- Rudder and tiller showing no cracks or splits?

You can learn to look over practically everything in the boat while you're cleaning up at the end of the day, without really adding much time to the process. Do it, and avoid the disappointment of problems when next you go out.

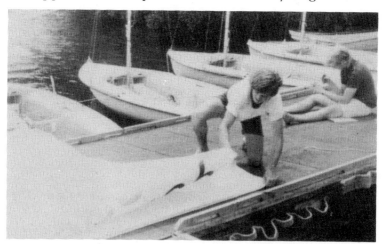

Take a little care when stowing your sails — proper folding produces faster sails by avoiding wrinkles which might interfere with efficient airflow over the sails' surfaces.

Check the boat *when you start out* on race day. If you possibly can, plan an extra ten minutes (which is more than you need) just to be sure that everything's right. Most of that extra time will be relaxation time, in which you can smile to yourself knowing your boat's all ready to go—it will put you in a much better racing mood.

●Sails set up right? Halyards OK, with cleats set up properly? Outhaul right for the wind? Boom downhaul and vang set? Jibsheet fairleads right?

● Stopper knots on the ends of the sheets, traveler lines, other working lines, so they can't get away from you? (Use a "figure-eight" knot; it's bigger than an "overhand" knot, and doesn't jam.)

● Rudder and tiller secure? Centerboard moving freely?

● Wind pennants OK, moving freely and where you can see them?

● All movable items (tools, charts, bailers, paddles) where they'll stay put and out of the way?

● All lines free of kinks, coiled, clear?

● Emergency kit complete and handy (wire, tape, sail patch, and first-aid items)?

● Stopwatch wound and working?

● DO YOU KNOW THE COURSE AND THE STARTING SIGNALS?

Once you've been through your checkout routine, forget about the boat and equipment, relax, and get ready to think only about the race.

2

Sailboat handling for speed in racing

Part of sailboat racing is, naturally, making the boat go as fast as possible. This is a matter of skill which can only be learned through experience. In the long run, the best way to learn to sail fast is to do a great deal of sailing, especially in races, where you'll learn quickly enough if someone else is going faster, and where you can watch what the others do differently from you.

Watch and learn. When the boat nearest to you is pulling away, try to see if the crew is sitting in a different part of the boat than yours are, look for any difference in the way his sails are set, watch his tiller to see if he has a trick about working the boat through waves, see if you can tell if his centerboard is in a different position from yours—try to *find out what he's doing differently*, and copy him if you can.

The things that you can do the most about, to make the boat go faster, are:

- Placing your weight so the boat's hull is most efficient in the water.
- Setting your sails to get the most out of them.
- Trimming your centerboard for best efficiency.
- Steering efficiently.
- Choosing the best course, considering wind puffs, waves, tides, and currents.

This chapter has a section on each of these things.

Right.
Boat kept flat has symmetrical wetted surface.
Note neutral helm (nearly straight rudder); no turning thrust.

Wrong.
Heeled boat with unsymmetrical wetted surface.
Note sharply-angled rudder (heavy weather helm) needed to offset turning hull thrust.

Personal weight and trimming the boat

The smaller the boat, the more important it is that you place your weight properly within it. In a typical 14- to 18-foot sloop, moving your weight only a foot or so fore or aft can make a very important difference in the boat's speed through the water.

Most small boats sail best with your weight near the center; if your weight is too far back, the transom (flat stern) will drag in the water—which really slows the boat, especially in light air. Get your weight at least far enough forward so that the bottom of the transom just kisses the water. Try experimenting some afternoon, sailing alongside another boat of the same class; you should be able to find the right place for your weight for best speed, and don't worry if that spot seems to be so far forward that the boat feels as if it's down in front—it's probably right (as long as you're not so far forward that the boat tries to nose under).

Personal weight and hiking the boat

With only a few exceptions, racing boats sail best when the mast is straight up. If you're one of the many skippers who doesn't feel he's going anywhere unless the boat is heeled over so the gunwale's in the water, try to remember it's not how you feel that counts, but how your boat feels the water. Most modern hulls were designed to be most efficient when they're flat, not when they're tipped over on their ears.

Since your boat was probably designed to be sailed "straight up," one of the biggest parts of your job when racing is to see to it that it *stays* flat—that is, straight up. In a blow, this is downright hard work. If you want to win races, you will want to learn how best to use your weight to hold the boat flat. This is called "hiking."

Hiking is illegal in cruising class boats—rule #66 says no one's torso may be outboard of the lifelines. And a number of other classes of boats (for example the super hot E-22) prohibit any kind of hiking assist—which excludes not only hiking straps and trapezes, but even handholds which would enable crew to lean outboard. Even on such boats,

Close-up of hiking straps; in this position skipper is comfortable while hanging most of his weight even farther outboard than illustrated

though, you can be sure that everyone is as far to windward as he can sit.

The basic thing to remember about hiking is that the farther your weight is located outboard of the centerline of the boat, the more it will work to keep the boat flat: the harder it blows, the farther out you move. If you have hiking straps in the boat, tuck your toes under them and get the rest of you as far out as it will go. Don't lie sideways on the rail—most of your weight is above your hips, so leaning your upper body outside the rail gives better leverage than having all of your body on the rail.

4 ft.

6⁺ ft.

This skipper, properly hiked, had his center of gravity outside the hull.

The crew, fully extended on the trapeze wire, has his center of gravity more than 50% farther out!

If there's a limit as to how far out you can lean without losing the tiller, then you need a tiller extension; if they're not legal in your class boat, see if tying the end of the mainsheet to the tiller won't serve.

If your boat's class rules permit, you may have a "trapeze" on which your crew can climb right out over the side of the boat; that's tricky until you get the knack—have someone show you how, and don't forget a life jacket.

When you first start learning to hike, take it easy and make sure some part of you is well enough anchored inside the boat so that you can get back in quickly. Lots of boats capsize to windward because everyone's stuck out over the side when the wind suddenly stops blowing hard.

There are a couple of fancy points about weight distribution. Sometimes, running downwind, you will find the boat "wallowing" (rolling from side to side), which is bad because it shakes the wind out of the sails, and may at moments leave you without enough rudder in the water for control. In such cases (assuming there are two or more of you on the boat), you may spread your weight away from the centerline of the boat—one moving to windward, the other balancing to leeward—which will keep the boat trimmed the same fore-and-aft, but with a higher *moment of inertia*, reducing the wallowing.

You should also consider inertia's effect on the fore-and-aft (pitching, or hobbyhorse) motion of the boat through waves: the boat should be encouraged to let its bow ride up and down on waves—otherwise, it will have to do extra work to plow through them. You can encourage this by concentrating your weight as near to the center as possible, where its moment of inertia is small, rather than having crew forward and skipper aft, which would produce moment that interferes with easy pitching.

> *Do* spread weight athwartships to reduce wallowing.
> *Don't* spread weight fore-and-aft to interfere with rocking.
> *And,* especially in larger boats, try to mount or store equipment as close to the center of the boat as you can; this will reduce its moment, making the boat livelier. For example, two anchors stored midships weigh the same and affect trim the same as if they were stored one for-

ward, one aft—but their moment will be much less. Two pounds of equipment atop a thirty-foot mast have the same moment (resistive effect to boat movement) as twelve pounds only five feet up.

Weight centered, this see-saw rocks fast and easily.

Weight spread apart, this see-saw goes much more slowly.

This crew and skipper are comfortably seated — and close together; their boat wallows.

With their weight hiked out, the wallowing is greatly reduced.

Setting your sails for best speed

One of the things that's most important in racing is *constant* attention to the set of your sails. You may be used to taking the boat out, cleating the sheets, and enjoying a nice, long ride without further attention to the sheets, but when you're racing, it's going to be different. The winning skipper will change his sails' settings for every little change in the *direction* of the wind and for every little change in the *strength* of the wind.

The general principle for sail setting is that the sail should (for any given course except close-hauled) be *as far out as possible without causing the sail to luff.*

On most modern boats, it turns out that the jib is more important than the mainsail, so check first to see that the jib is trimmed its best: holding your course steady, ease the sheet slowly out until you catch the first signs of luffing (wrinkling flutter at the front edge of the sail), then tighten the sheet just enough to make the luffing stop.

This mainsail is pictured with exaggerated luffing — *that is, the sail is collapsing/fluttering in forward areas — indicating that it is set too nearly head-to-wind. Beginners are often confused by* leaching — *that is, fluttering on the after edge of the sail.*

If you don't have a jib, set the mainsail in the same way as if it were a jib—ease it until you see the first sign of luffing, then haul it back in enough to stop the luff.

If you have a genoa jib, which overlaps the mainsail, setting the main is going to be a bit harder because it will often get some backwind from the jib when sailing close-hauled. "Backwinding" refers to wind that has already been across the jib and gets funneled into the forward, lee side of the mainsail. This backwind will cause the mainsail to luff, even when it's properly set, and there's nothing that can be done about it.

With a main that's being backwinded, you'll have to do some trial-and-error work to find out just how much luffing

on your particular heading is caused by the backwind, fix
that amount of luffing in your mind, then set the sail as
far out as it will go without increasing the area of sail that
is luffing. To learn how much area of the mainsail luffs
from backwind, simply work the sail in and out a foot or
so—you'll quickly see that there's a fixed amount of luffing
that doesn't change much, which is the backwind area.

Something to watch: the amount of luffing area from
backwind varies with the strength of the wind as well as with
how near to close-hauled you're sailing. The stronger the
:wind, the larger the area of backwind you'll get; in very
light airs, it will go down to very little or no backwinded
area.

too close; mainsail is   *jib sheet eased slightly;*   *sheets eased further for*
backwinded   *both sails have good shape*   *full curves on light-air*
                                                                day

When close-hauled, you already know that you want to set
the sails as close to the boat as you can, then steer the boat
as close to the wind as you can without luffing. Following
the same principles as in sail setting, if you have a jib, that's
the sail to watch for the first signs of luffing. First, sheet
the jib in, then set your course as close to the wind as you
can without luffing the jib; then sheet your main as far as
is necessary to stop it from luffing (once again, ignoring
any backwinded area).

The strength of the wind *and* the speed of the boat determine how hard in you can sheet your sails when close-

hauled. In strong winds, sheet your jib in just as tight as you can. In lighter winds, sheet it in until you see it beginning to lose that nice airfoil (airplane wing-shaped curve) up front—too flat a sail isn't efficient in light airs. In very light airs, leave it loose enough to have a nice fat belly curve —which means sheets about three inches looser than tight close-hauled.

Your boat may allow for changing the fore-and-aft location of the jibsheet fairleads. If so, this will be an important adjustment, particularly if you carry a relatively large jib. The correct setting of the fairleads is something you're going to have to learn by trial and error, and since it will vary with the strength of the wind, you should keep experimenting with the setting every time you sail. Keep something on the boat with which to mark the settings you decide are best. (Plastic electrician's tape works fine.)

Jibsheet blocks, mounted on tracks, may be adjusted fore-and-aft which varies the angle of downward effort; moving blocks forward causes the jibsheet to exert more downward pull, which in turn flattens the upper part of the jib preventing premature luffing in the upper portion of the sail, and moving blocks aft "opens" the upper roach, preventing premature luffing in the lower part of the jib. Blocks should be adjusted so that the jib luffs evenly over its entire height; then, set blocks farther aft in heavy winds. (Note markings on the track, helping crew to repeat best settings discovered through trial-and-error.)

The way to set the fairleads is to get the boat close-hauled and sailing fast, then ease into the wind, watching for the first signs of luffing on the jib. You'll quickly find that the jib always begins to luff first at some particular point on the sail. If the luff area is the upper half of the jib or higher, set the jib sheet fairlead farther forward; if the luff first shows up much below the diagonal seam, set the fairlead farther aft.

If your boat is equipped with Barber haulers (which move the jib leads inboard and outboard), the principle is: let them outboard except when close-hauled in a good breeze—then bring them inboard to permit pointing closer to the wind. If the water is rough, get them back outboard some, to get better "power."

When setting the mainsail for close-hauled work there's a handy rule of thumb: sheet the main in until the point where further pulling makes the boom come downward rather than inward, then let it back out an inch. In very light winds, let it out another four or five inches; in very heavy winds, haul it in as tight as you can. (When pulling the main in so tight as to pull the boom downward, you see, it flattens the curves in the sail; a flat sail is good in heavy winds, but you need fuller curves in light air.)

Here's a fine point about setting sails when close-hauled: the faster the boat is going, the closer you can afford to set the sails. So, if your boat slows down from hitting waves, or from tacking, ease the sails out an inch or so farther than they were until the boat gets back up to speed, then haul things back tight.

In this position, most pull is downward; more effort will only flatten the sail.

In this position, pull on mainsheet is mostly inward; more pull will trim sail closer inboard.

When reaching or running downwind, you know that the mainsail blankets the jib, so at this point the mainsail becomes the more important of the two. Set the mainsail first, following the same rule of putting it out as far as you can until you see it luff, then hauling it back in just enough to stop the luff. Once the main is set properly, do the best you can with the jib. If it won't draw well on the same side as the main, feel free to *wing it* (setting the jib on the opposite side from the main). Once out on the wind, the same old rule fits the jib—out until it luffs, back enough to stop the luff.

Jib set behind mainsail may be blanketed; placing jib in "wing-and-wing" position gets it into clear air.

(Keep trimming the jib sheet more or less all the time—but especially when the jib is "winged out." Test and retest every minute or so to be sure that the sail is just inside the point of luffing; this really makes a difference in the boat's speed.) *Note*: when the jib is winged, you may be able to "feed" it wind by sheeting the main in a bit farther than you would otherwise think is right, which will spill wind forward, past the mast, and onto the jib. While this costs you something in lost efficiency of the main, it's worth it if that's what it takes to get your jib pulling. When you're doing this, *watch out for an accidental jibe* of the main.

Mainsail sheeted in slightly feeds air to the jib.

If you have a spinnaker, you can get it working for you any time the apparent wind is abeam or farther aft. (Apparent wind, you remember, is the wind the boat feels including the effect produced by its own forward motion—apparent wind is, naturally, farther forward than the true wind any-time the boat is moving forward.) Some of the new spin-naker designs are effective with the wind well forward of the beam.

The rule for setting the spinnaker is still the same—slack off (on the downwind sheet) until the sail starts to luff, then back until it stops. The windward guy—the one to the spin-naker pole—should be hauled in as tight as possible without causing the sail to collapse.

With a spinnaker drawing, it's more important than the main, so sail to keep the spinnaker full first, worry about the main last.

Keeping track of the wind

You can't expect to keep your sails pulling at their very best possible setting all of the time if you don't know where the wind is all of the time. Wind has a funny way of chang-ing direction, at least a little, nearly every minute, and you should be adjusting your sails to almost every little shift. It's very helpful to have some *wind pennants,* or *telltales* around the boat, which will tell you very quickly when there's any change in the wind. Make sure you have one or more, and keep your eyes on them.

Remember that the wind pennant sees the *apparent* wind, not the true wind, so it's not telling where the wind is really coming from, but only what wind results when you add the boat's forward motion to the force of the real wind. Remember, too, that it's hard to find a place to put a wind pennant where the wind that reaches it won't get deflected from the sails, the mast, or some other part of the boat. Still, you can count on the wind pennant telling you when there's a change in the wind.

The usual minimum for wind pennants is: a couple of pieces of knitting yarn tied to the outer shrouds. Some kind of pennant at the top of the mast is nice, especially down-wind (where the wind bouncing off the mainsail makes yarn on the shrouds nearly useless). In really light, drifting airs, there's nothing like smoke to show you the wind. If you don't smoke tobacco, carry some sticks of punk (you can still find it at the incense counter in "import" stores). On drizzly days, when feathers and yarn get useless from the wet, try using magnetic tape from a tape recorder.

Positioning your centerboard

(If you sail a keel boat, skip this section.)

The general idea about changing the position of your centerboard is this: since the centerboard may amount to a third or more of all the surface of the boat in the water, and all underwater surface counts as resistance, you want to keep the least amount of centerboard in the water that you can. *You need only enough board in the water to keep the boat from making leeway (that is, moving sidewise).* The amount of centerboard that this requires varies with two things: (1) the faster the boat is moving the less board you need; and (2) the closer-hauled your sails are set the more board you need.

A simple general statement about how to set your board would say: close-hauled (beating to windward) the board should be all the way down; on courses that are ten or more degrees off close-hauled, and farther off the wind to courses where the apparent wind is on the beam, you should be able to lift your board between 15 and 30 percent —that is, two thirds or more of the board still in the water—depending upon how fast you're going (and if things are really roaring, a good planing wind, you might be able to get away with only half the board) on up to about 50 percent board on a beam reach. As your course moves farther downwind so that the apparent wind is clearly coming from behind the beam, you should be able to ease the board farther up until none of it's in the water. Running dead before the wind, most boats need some centerboard in the water—about one quarter of it—to counteract the torque (twisting pressure) on the boat when your sail is way out to the side.

It's easy to learn how much centerboard you need at any time. Watch your wake, while holding the boat on a steady course; if the wake is going off at an angle, it means that

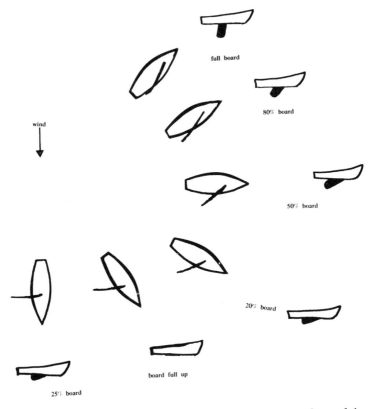

wind

full board

80% board

50% board

20% board

board full up

25% board

the boat is sideslipping, and you need more centerboard in the water. Try easing the board up until you notice signs of sideslipping, then ease just enough back in the water to straighten out the wake. If in doubt, put a little more board into the water—better too much than too little board in the water.

Some fine points about setting the centerboard:

• *Wallowing*: often, sailing fairly well before the wind, you'll find the boat rolling from side to side. Get some more of the board down, all of it if need be, to stop the rolling. Rolling hurts speed more than too much board in the water.
• *Weather helm*: if you have a pivoting centerboard—one that swings up toward the stern as distinguished from a daggerboard which moves straight up and down—you

should try lifting it *just a little* (5 to 10 percent) on those close-hauled courses with a strong wind where you find yourself dragging the rudder through the water sideways to keep the boat from rounding up into the wind. Depending on the shape and rig of your boat, this may move the *center of resistance* of the boat far enough back to take the pressure off your rudder without causing too much sideslipping. This is something to try when you're fooling around until you learn the effect—not for the first time in an important race.

• *Following seas*: when being chased by big waves, the boat sometimes decides to do a foolish thing like suddenly swing around a half-turn. If this happens in a good blow with most or all of your centerboard down, the boat may "trip" sidewise on the board leading to instant-get-wet. Pulling the board up makes it easier for the boat to skitter sideways rather than trip.

A final word about the board: *always have the board at least part way down before any major maneuver* is tried. Make it a completely automatic routine to down the board before turning at a mark of the course, before jibing, before doing anything that requires much rudder movement. The boat needs the sidewise resistance of the centerboard in order to turn well. (But when jibing in a blow, don't use any more board than you need for control, so as to avoid the risk of "tripping.")

Any time you're close beside a boat with luffing rights on you, you're in big danger of having to move fast; keep your centerboard down, or at the very least have it ready to go down the instant his does. Keep this in mind when you read the rules section on luffing.

Planing and surfing

You probably already understand that all boats have what amounts to a speed limit on how fast they can go while their hulls are "in" the water. This *hull speed* varies with a number of things like design shape, sail area, weight, and most of all, the length of waterline. However, the limit on the boat's speed goes out the window whenever the hull gets up on top of the water, *planing*—skimming along the surface like a speedboat.

Most modern, small racing boats are designed with hull shapes that will plane very easily—and almost any light boat will do it if the wind's blowing hard enough.

Racers *have* to learn how to help their boats get planing, since the difference in possible speed is just tremendous. A typical small boat may have a hull speed limit around 4 to 5 knots, for instance, yet it won't be unusual to clock the same boat at speeds of 8, 10, 12, or more knots when planing in a good blow.

Planing and *surfing* are both cases of the boat skimming on top of the water, with no hull limit; the difference is that *planing* is the skimming action caused by a nice blow of wind (and it may just go on and on while the wind lasts), while *surfing* is what we call a nice but brief ride that's caused by riding downhill on waves partly propelled by the forward motion of surface water on the wave form.

In either case, what you have to learn is how to help the boat get started—then hang on for the ride!

When will the boat plane? It depends on the boat, of course, and the weight it's carrying. (The first thing you can do to help the boat plane in lighter winds is get skinny—carry the least weight you can manage for the winds.) Look for planing any time the wind is 15 knots or so, if you have a good planing boat, and when the wind is coming from about the beam (sidewise to the boat) or farther aft. Better planing boats will plane with the wind a bit farther forward, and the harder it's blowing, the closer to the wind you can plane. Some of the hottest boats will plane in a good blow when they're practically close-hauled; if you've got such a boat, do some experimenting to learn whether the boat might not get to windward faster by sailing not quite close-hauled, and giving up a few degrees of pointing toward the wind in exchange for the extra speed of planing.

How do we set the boat up for planing? If it's a good planing boat, sailing on a broad reach or downwind and in a good blow, you won't have to worry about it—it'll plane. Your job is to learn how to help the boat get started when there's only barely enough wind for planing. Here are some of the things to do:

● Set the boat on the best course you can find for planing—on most boats, about 15 to 30 degrees farther downwind than a beam reach.

● Get the centerboard up as high as conditions permit—hopefully, at least halfway up.

● Get the boat as flat as you possibly can—most boat designs will plane much sooner when not heeling at all.

● *Quickly,* move your weight back a little, and at the same time trim the sails in a bit—this does several things at once:

> it gets the boat's nose out of the water, ready to climb up on top of the water;
>
> it gives your boat a little extra shove forward for an instant, in reaction to the *lunge* of your weight and the *pump* of the sail; and
>
> it gets the sails set for the wind shift of the apparent wind (as the boat picks up planing speed, its increased forward motion will make the wind seem to come from farther forward).

● If you can time it right, make all those moves at the same time you steer the boat to slide down the front edge of a wave.

If it works, you'll know it—the boat will really surge ahead, nearly double its speed right away. If it doesn't work, set things up and try again. Try changing the boat's course a little more downwind next time, or a little closer to abeam of the wind. Practice, you'll get the feel after a while.

What can you do to keep the boat planing? First, do be

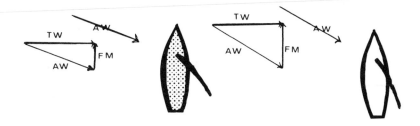

The spotted boat, not planing, has apparent wind just forward of the beam. The white boat, on a plane, is going nearly twice as fast and has apparent wind farther forward and stronger. (FM = forward motion; TW = true wind; AW = apparent wind.)

alert for the apparent wind shifting forward; the boat goes so much faster when planing that its forward motion noticeably affects the apparent wind and you will have to trim sails closer in than for the same course when not planing. In a really good planing situation, a course nearly 90 degrees across the *true* wind may require sails trimmed to just about close-hauled.

Second, do everything you can to keep the boat flat to sustain planing; many boats simply don't plane when heeled, and just about all plane better when flat.

Third, move your weight far enough forward to keep the boat flat in the fore-and-aft plane; you probably lunged aft to help the boat get started (by pulling its nose out of the water). If you stay back, you'll be dragging the boat's stern.

> *Note*: The proper place to keep your weight will be different when planing. Your weight (combination skipper and crew) was probably best right near the middle when not planing. Now that you're planing, the right place is likely a foot or two farther aft. Experiment; you want to trim with the bow just clear of the water.
>
> *Note*: Watch out you don't get caught hiking the boat too far to windward. The amount of hiking (extending body weight out on the windward side to balance the heeling tendency) that's needed to keep the boat flat is less when planing than at lower speeds—so be ready to come in a bit the moment the boat takes off on a plane.

Watch out for the waves. In winds that are barely strong enough to sustain planing, you'll kill your forward speed if you let the bow go plunging into the waves. Try to keep the boat moving sidewise on the downhill side of waves. (See the section on surfing that follows.)

Trim the centerboard as high as you dare; when the boat is flying on a plane, you don't need much board (if any) to avoid sideslipping—but you may need some to keep things under control.

How about *surfing*? Surfing is really a special case of planing, and nearly everything we've said about planing applies to surfing—except in this case, we're working the downhill side of waves as our booster, instead of an extra bit of wind.

Waves go faster than you can and the surface water is

moving forward on the front of each wave, so if you can catch a ride on one, you'll pick up speed. There's a knack to catching the waves, and you'll get it with practice. The best advice I can pass along is that of Sunfish champion Tom Burke: "When you see a hole in the water, steer for it; then try to keep the boat level (to the water you're on, not to the horizon). Be ready to move around a lot and in a hurry—if the bow starts to go under, jump back to bounce it out; if a wave starts to bump your stern, jump on the bow."

If the waves are farther apart from crest to crest than the length of your boat, you should be able to hang onto the forward edge of a given wave for quite a while. If you start to outrun the wave (threatening to nose into the uphill side of the one ahead), steer off at an angle of 10 to 20 degrees, slowing down just enough to get back onto the downslope. If the wave starts to get ahead of you, steer a course that's directly with the wave direction, so that the boat gets the greatest possible push, which may get you back onto the downslope—and if not, it will help the next wave to catch up with you in the least possible distance of sailing.

A special note about the racing rules. The rules very specifically *do* allow lunging, and trimming the sails, and so forth for the purpose of *starting* the boat to plane, but it's not legal to keep doing those things once planing begins, *and* it's very much *not legal* to do those things for any reason except to promote planing (or surfing).

3

Helmsmanship

This chapter is on *how* to steer for fast sailing—not on when and where to steer, which comes under "tactics."

Sloppy work on the helm can kill your boat—good work keeps it sailing fast and smoothly throughout its maneuvers. The first key to good helmsmanship is *smoothness*.

Too sharp a movement of the rudder kills the boat's way through the water;
too slow a rudder movement exposes the boat to going into irons when tacking, or to dragging out a maneuver (like a jibe) that ought to take only a couple of seconds, or leaves a hole in space for your competitor to slip by.

Movement of your weight in the boat must also be smooth, and there's a terrific tendency to go thumping around when handling helm and lines, so when you're practicing helmsmanship, keep in mind that any body movement that you can feel through the hull is too rough. The lighter the air, the more important it is to move smoothly; in drifting conditions, slither around the boat like a snake.

We'll look at helmsmanship in terms of the basic kinds of maneuvers:
tacking
jibing
handling knock-down puffs
beating into waves
riding with waves

Before going into the specific maneuvers, let's be sure that you understand the reasons for keeping the helm movements smooth. You know that the rudder turns the boat because the water going by the rudder pushes against it. And since you know that, you surely appreciate that the faster the boat is moving through the water, the less turn of the tiller is required to get the same rate of turning of the boat. (And, obviously, if the boat isn't moving at all, then no amount of rudder movement will cause the boat to turn at all.)

What you have next to think about is that, if the rudder is turned too far, the water won't flow past it smoothly, but will become turbulent at the rudder, causing a very high amount of drag and actually decreasing the turning effect of the rudder.

And, similarly, if the boat is being turned too fast, the underwater parts (of the centerboard, keel, everything) start to skid sideways through the water, and once again may create turbulence and drag . . . plus a higher than usual rate of sideslip, which ends up as being movement in a direction that you don't want.

The trick to good helmsmanship is to avoid these kinds of turbulence, drag, and slip, and to keep the boat moving smoothly through the water, with the nicest, smoothest flow of water that's possible—turning smoothly in an arc rather than jerking around at an angle.

If you move the rudder with a jerk, rather than easing it into the right angle, you'll create a little eddy (turbulence) at the rudder blade, and (even though not noticed) others along all the other underwater parts of the boat—all costing you speed which you can't spare.

Since your sailboat changes speed as you tack, or round a mark, the smooth helmsman will find that there is a constant change in the "right amount" of rudder as he goes through the maneuver—rudder increasing as speed decreases.

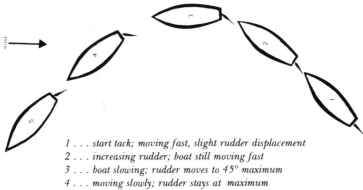

1 . . . start tack; moving fast, slight rudder displacement
2 . . . increasing rudder; boat still moving fast
3 . . . boat slowing; rudder moves to 45° maximum
4 . . . moving slowly; rudder stays at maximum
5 . . . coming out onto new course; rudder being centered smoothly

Tacking

Tacking right, in a small boat, won't cost much time or speed—for a rule of thumb, figure on losing about one half of a boat length's distance for each tack you make. It will be a little less on a good tack with decent wind and not much roughness to the water, and a bit more in very light winds or very rough water.

Some rules for good tacking:
1. Always be ready for a sudden tack—there's no excuse in the world for having to do any preparation after you decide to tack and before you can begin the maneuver. Your crew is entitled to know you're going around, but the old routine of "ready about . . . (pause) . . . hard-a-lee" is nonsense in any boat under forty feet. Both you and your crew should have all lines and whatnot ready for the next tack first thing after finishing the last one. Then, simply saying "tacking" as you start the maneuver should be all that your crew needs to hear. *Exception*: if your crew is out on a trapeze, he needs some notice; find out how much, and don't forget it.
2. Ease the tiller into the turn, then smoothly increase the amount of rudder as the boat slows down while turning,

and finally ease the rudder back to normal for the new tack —always smoothly. The right amount of rudder for most boats is around 45 degrees, increasing to a maximum of 60 degrees if the boat's going slowly or has to crash through heavy waves. You should never need more than 60 degrees of rudder unless the boat's going into irons—more rudder turn than that and you'll be dragging a nearly flat blade behind the boat—great for quick stops at the mooring, but lousy for moving a boat in a race.

If there isn't a rule against it in your class, rig up a tiller stop so that you'll get the right amount of rudder simply by letting go of the tiller—then your hands are free to switch the main sheet and move into the new hiking position, picking up the tiller as you're ready to stop the turn. Even in the little boats, like dinghies and boardboats, you can get the effect of a tiller stop by keeping tension on the mainsheet as you tack, which keeps the traveler rig tight enough to catch and stop the tiller before it turns too far.

3. Keep the mainsail drawing as much as you can, for as long as you can. When you start the turn, haul in on the mainsheet any last little bit you can, to keep it driving for the last second, and keep the mainsheet tight all the way through the maneuver until it's drawing on the new tack, then ease it out as you settle onto course to avoid pinching it.

Remember, the proper close-hauled setting for sails is a bit tighter when the boat's moving fast than when moving slowly. Since you've lost some speed in tacking, the proper setting for the main (and jib) when you first assume the course for the new tack will be a couple of inches farther out than it was on the old tack. Then, as the boat picks up speed, the sails get trimmed in to their high-speed position.

4. Follow the wind with the jib. The jib should be kept on the cleat, indeed, sheeted in a little tighter as you start the tack if that's possible, to make it draw until the last possible moment. Then, the instant the jib starts luffing, it should be cast off the cleat and allowed to weathervane across as the bow swings through the wind. Make your crew practice setting the jib sheet on the new tack just at the instant it can first fill, and not a moment before.

The usual boo-boos are, (a) casting off the jib the moment you say "tacking," which wastes half-a-second's sail drive, (b)

wind

RIGHT

1. "Hard-a-lee", tack starts both sails drawing well.

2. Main sheet tight, jib luffing free, sheet cast off.

3. Jib carried across, following the wind as boat rounds.

4. Jib sheet hauled.

5. All sheets cleated, sails full, tack completed.

WRONG

1. Jib sheet cast off too soon (before first luff)

2. Jib carried across bow too soon, backwinding.

3. Jib cleated too soon still backwinding

4. Tack complete, speed and distance lost

dragging the jib across to the new tack faster than the boat is swinging, which causes the jib to backwind, thus resisting the boat's turning, or (c) setting the jibsheet too soon, also causing backwinding (sometimes to the extent of forcing the boat into irons).   Train your crew to watch out for tacks that aren't going off right, threatening to leave the boat in irons. A crew that knows the danger and has his head up will spot the danger before it's serious and pull the jib back to the old leeward side, catching the wind on the back of the jib and forcing the boat over onto the new tack with backwind . . . and then when the boat is around, he will move fast to get the jib drawing on the new tack. If you can't teach him that, you can at least teach him to do it on your command of "backwind," and *you* watch for the danger.

*Deliberate backwinding of the jib (in second position)
forces completion of the tack after
the boat threatens to stop head-to-wind.*

5. Practice. Practice and practice tacking. When you're good at it, you'll make half-a-length to a full length per tack on most of your opponents, and that comes to between three and ten lengths even on short courses. And until you're confident that you can pull off a fast tack without killing the boat, you really can't get into some of the games we'll discuss under Tactics.

Jibing

Jibing is harder to mess up than tacking, except when it's blowing hard—then you have to look out or you'll break something (or capsize).

The helmsmanship part of steering for the jibe is duck soup in light air—just start turning toward the new course smoothly and slowly, have your crew get a good hold on the boom, and when it's ready to swing, swing the boom back hard by hand, forcing it past the centerline and keep on moving it until the wind takes it. Then let the sheet run out slowly, so the sail is drawing as it goes the rest of the way out to its setting on the new tack. When done right, the sail will only be out of wind for about a quarter of the trip from side to side, and the crew's weight will move smoothly at the same time, keeping the boat flat throughout the maneuver. You'll generally do best keeping the skipper midships and steady, only moving to help keep the boat flat when the crew can't keep it flat alone.

The crew has to know when the sail's ready to be put over—and if you can't trust him to know, teach him to swing it on your command. The right time is the first moment that you're sure it will stay put on the other tack and that you're sure you're strong enough to swing it. If in doubt, watch for the roach of the sail to start flopping—then she'll go.

If you don't have a boom vang keeping downward pressure on the boom, make sure that when the crew swings the boom, he also pulls downward on it as hard as he can. That keeps the roach from sagging off (danger of goosewinging) and makes the sail kick the boat forward a bit as it's swung aft.

In heavy air, jibing is hairier. Dangers: goosewing, capsize, or damage to shrouds, spreaders, and mainsheet rigging.

"Goosewinging" refers to the situation in which the bottom part of the sail jibes properly, but the upper part of the sail gets left on the old side. A common result is a torn sail; other possible results include damaged standing rigging, even dismasting. The way to prevent it is to keep downward pressure on the boom, since the boom has to rise quite a bit in order to leave enough slack in the sail to sag into a goosewing. If you have a boom vang, and it's set up tight, no problem; otherwise, your crew should keep downward pressure on the boom whenever it's all the way out, and especially when jibing.

Uncontrolled jibe . . . as the boat sails through the wind direction, the boom rises and the sail flops; after the jibe, the upper portion of the sail may be left on the (now) windward side, forming "goosewing".

The danger of capsize comes up whenever the sail is holding wind and the crew isn't in position to hike properly. You're tempting the situation in a blow when your crew goes to leeward to grab the boom for the jibe; and you're in danger if the sail grabs wind on the new tack, after jibing, before you're all set to hike. The cure, in each case, is mainsheet control. Jibing in a strong wind, haul the main in most or all of the way before steering toward the new-tack course. Indeed, luff a bit toward the wind in order to prevent an accidental early jibe; then, when the boom is close aboard, swing the boat over toward the new course. As soon as the sail swings, let the mainsheet out fast, fast enough to keep the sail from grabbing much wind until it's most or all of the way out. Oversteer a bit, toward the new windward side, to keep the sail from flinging up against the shrouds and spreader. Then, when things are under control and you're ready to hike, you can simultaneously bear off onto the new course and sheet the sail into good trim.

The same kinds of controlled maneuvering will prevent other damage dangers which come up when the sail swings violently in a blow.

Controlled jibe used in heavy wind: steer to windward enough to avoid premature jibe while sheeting the main (1,2); then, steer through the wind direction as the main jibes, letting the mainsheet out rapidly (3).

Handling the jib when jibing is easier, because it doesn't matter much; just be sure to get the pole off, if you have it spritted, and swing it over as soon as you know the mainsail jibe didn't go wrong. The jib is so relatively poor on a downwind run that until you're really expert, the right thing to do about it is to forget it; ten seconds one way or the other really won't make much difference, as long as the main's handled right.

If you have a spinnaker flying, that's different. It's your important sail going downwind, so jibe it first, and then worry about your main—but try to get your main moving in time to be sure that it won't blanket and collapse the chute. There are tons of techniques written up for jibing spinnakers, which is hard to do right on big boats. On small boats, this will do:

1. Send the crew forward, skipper balancing and preparing to sheet in the main.
2. Crew takes pole off the mast and snaps clew (leeward corner of chute) to the pole, which leaves you with both corners on the pole; skipper starts bringing in the main.

3. Unsnap the former tack of the chute from pole which now becomes the clew (new leeward corner); skipper jibes the main, and crew sets pole on the mast.

4. Trim chute and main at the same time to the new course. The skipper probably has to work with the tiller between his knees, and he surely has to balance the boat, since the crew will be trapped by the main.

Don't forget to get your centerboard down enough for effective steering before jibing.

1 . . . ready to jibe.
2 . . . spinnaker man takes pole off mast.
3 . . . pole clipped to (former) clew, which now becomes tack.
4 . . . former tack let go from pole, becomes clew.
5 . . . pole back on mast.

How to steer in waves

Whenever the waves are high enough to slow or swing the boat, you have to start making compromises for fastest sailing and best course. We'll examine first the general principles, then look separately at the problems of going *into* waves and of going *with* waves.

You've got to remember that sharp rudder movements create dragging turbulence, and excessive rudder creates a flat, braking surface which stops the boat. On the other hand, waves tend to throw the boat off course. Therefore, you're always faced with the trade-off problem of letting the waves swing the boat, or of using a lot of rudder work to hold the boat on course. The lighter the boat, the more effect the waves have. The fastest sailing will come out of helmsmanship which uses moderate rudder movements and allows moderate course displacement.

Going into waves gets to be a problem, because the techniques vary with the size and shape of the waves.

sail nearly straight up big waves so boat's bow can split the water, minimizing the blow that the boat receives from the wave

wave crests

gather speed on the downhill side and between crests

On long, gradually sloped waves, fall off the wind a bit when you're sailing up the waves, which will help keep the boat moving on its uphill ride; then when going downhill, you can afford to pinch up a bit closer into the wind.

On short, steep-sided waves, the technique is quite the opposite: try to get the boat as nearly head-on to the wave as you can manage just at the moment it hits, which allows the bow to cleave the water—minimizing the blow the boat receives from the wave, and recover speed by falling off a bit on the downhill side of the waves. In steep-sided chop, it's especially important to keep the boat as flat as possible when entering the waves—this helps to reduce the impact by letting the boat slip over the top a bit better.

Going with the waves, you have two separate problems to watch. One, your boat will try to submarine, sticking its nose under the uphill side of the wave in front of you. Two, whenever a following wave catches up with you, it wants to swing the stern around to the front, called *broaching*. You prevent submarining by steering a course a bit sidewise to the uphill side of waves you're catching up with, then after you're up on the wave, bringing the boat back to the course you want. In much the same way, you prevent broaching by turning a bit as the wave catches up to you, so that it hits squarely from behind. Get your centerboard up enough to permit some skidding if you do get turned.

In either case, if you're in surfing conditions, you'll probably already be going enough with the waves to prevent a need for radical steering. Remember to watch out for the unexpected accidental jibe that may be caused by a wave swinging the boat. (This can sneak up on you, because often a good surfing ride down a wave will get you going so fast that the apparent wind becomes next to nothing, and it doesn't much matter where it's from—until suddenly you come off the wave, the boat quits surfing and slows down, and *wham* comes the jibe.)

Sailing close to the wind

Beating to windward, the problem is to sail as close to the wind as you can without sacrificing speed. Here's the one single skill in sailboat racing that most often separates the leaders from the pack. Somehow, the hotshot seems always to point a little higher and move a little faster. There isn't any special secret to it—it's another case of making the best trade-off.

The general principles are easily listed; making them work out right is a matter of feel, developed through practice. Principles:

1. Set sail properly for close-hauled work—as close as you can haul in the boom without overly flattening the sail, a bit tighter in a blow than in light air. Rule of thumb on the jib is as tight as you can get it in heavy wind, and a tiny bit less (half-inch of sheet or so) to let some curve back into it in lighter airs. Rule of thumb on the main is: haul in until you see that the boom is going downward rather than inward, then let out just enough sheet (an inch or two in heavy airs, twice ɩhat in light) to make the curves smooth.
2. Sail as close to the wind as possible without luffing the jib.
3. Sail the boat flat, flat, flat.
4. Move weight far enough forward to keep the transom out of the water.
5. In heavy airs, spill wind rather than let the boat heel excessively. Heeling is certainly excessive if it's enough to make you carry a weather helm of more than 10 or

15 degrees. (That is, you have to keep the rudder at an angle to prevent the boat from rounding up into the wind.)

Most boats, when knocked on their sides, develop an extreme weather helm, making you drag the rudder along at 40, 50, or more degrees of turn; when this happens, the rudder "stalls," developing so much turbulence that it becomes almost totally ineffective—while creating a tremendous braking drag in the water.

Before this happens, you must spill enough wind to get the boat back on its feet, relieve the pressure on the rudder, and restore it to working effectiveness.

When you see a knockdown puff coming, anticipate it, pinching the boat up into the wind a bit extra, then standing ready to ease the sheets.

6. "Pinch" intermittently, and that only when the boat is moving fast. "Pinching" refers to sailing a little closer to the wind than normal—it gets you a little closer to where you want to go, but at the risk of sailing slower. Two things happen when the boat is pinched:

One, the force of the wind on the sails becomes more sideways, less forward, and this changed direction of effort becomes quite extreme over the last few degrees of course into the wind—therefore, the boat begins to slow down, simply because it gets a lot less forward drive out of the sails.

Two, both because of the slower forward motion and because of the greater sideways pressure, the boat begins to make more leeway (sideslipping) than before. You actually cross through a trade-off point, whereby for every extra degree toward the wind you sail, you actually pick up more than an extra degree of leeway—so you end up *pointing* closer to the wind, but actually *making good* through the water a course that is not so close to the wind. In some boats, with relatively undersized centerboards, the centerboard actually stalls (picking up turbulence that kills its effectiveness), at which point leeway becomes tremendous.

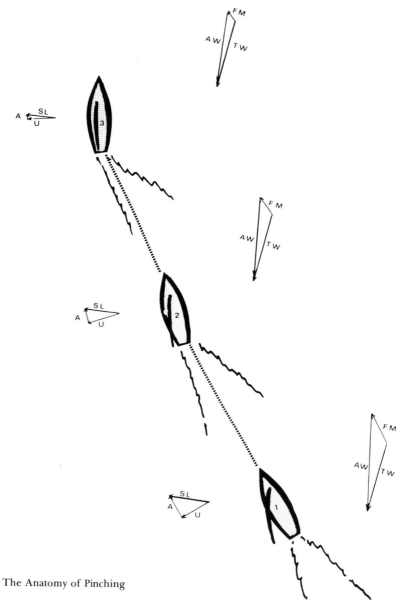

The Anatomy of Pinching

As the boat pinches (position 2) the sail's lift (SL on vector diagrams) becomes more useless effort to the side (U), and less advantage toward the intended course (A). Forward motion is reduced, although the apparent wind (AW) seems temptingly to have "lifted"; this leads to position 3, in which the apparent wind is not so strong, although the true wind is the same. In less apparent wind, SL is even weaker, and practically all lift is useless. Note the tell-tale crooked wake.

Conclusions: In light airs, pinching always hurts you, and you're better off sailing faster but not quite so close to the wind. In heavier airs, when the boat will go full speed anyway, you can afford to pinch up a bit until the boat begins to make leeway, then fall off to regain speed, then pinch, and so forth. This leads to sailing a scalloping course, much like the best way to sail into waves. Scallop into the wind on the puffs (avoiding the knockdowns), recover your course when the boat slows, and scallop up again.

Sailing in shifting winds

Wind doesn't know enough to stay steady, either in direction or in force. You must always be aware where the wind is from, and you must respond automatically to any of its changes.

Learn to spot the shifts before they hit you. They're usually easily visible, since the wind puff ruffles the water, and changes in either the direction or the strength of the wind cause color changes on the water. Puffs of stronger air look like wrinkly dark spots on the water, and you can watch them come down on you. The wind will hit you a couple of seconds before the color patch reaches you.

Direction shifts of the wind are harder to spot, though they may also change the color of the water a bit, by causing crosshatch ripples on the water. The easy way to spot coming direction changes is by watching what's going on with boats that are windward of you. (When *you're* in front, congratulations—just cover as described in the Tactics section.)

When there's a wind direction change that's detectable up ahead, sail on the tack that will get you to it soonest, if it's a favorable change, and latest if it isn't. It's worth making a tack to get a favorable wind shift early, or to stay away from an unfavorable shift. Many wind shifts are very temporary, and run down imaginary corridors, so you may completely hit or miss one, depending upon your luck and your success in chasing it.

When a wind direction change hits you, if it's a header (making what was a good course now a luffing course), then *tack*. Don't wait more than two seconds, to make sure it's sticking, then go over. If you're any good at tacking, you'll be around in three to five seconds; if the shift doesn't hold, you can always tack back and still be ahead of the game. The biggest mistake of the beginner is his reluctance to tack soon—presumably because he hasn't practiced enough to be sure he'll make the tack smoothly and quickly.

Tacking on wind shifts is very important—it's one of the great separators of men from boys.

Appendix D gives a full explanation of why, and how, to utilize "maxi-tack" for optimum performance going upwind.

Going downwind in variable-strength airs, stick with the old-timers' rule of sailing closer to the wind in the lulls, bearing off with the wind on the puffs. This has two advantages. One, your closer-to-the-wind course in lulls helps you go up to meet the next puff, getting it sooner, and by the same reasoning your bearing off in the puffs helps you stay with the puff longer, to your obvious advantage. Two, this sailing strategy has you sailing a closer-to-the-wind course (which is faster) in the lulls, when that's necessary to get best speed out of the boat, and has you on your slowest heading (running fuller before the wind) during the periods when the wind is best. The amount by which you can afford to change your course to play this game depends somewhat on how much difference there is between puffs and lulls (the more that difference, the more it's worth exaggerating the game). On average, sailing up about 10 to 15 degrees in the lulls, and then sailing below your base course the same amount in the puffs, is about right. If there isn't 30 to 40 percent difference or more between puffs and

fall off in puff;
ride down with it

lulls, forget it and sail your shortest course.

Note: There's an exception to this strategy—marginal planing weather. There will be days when the boat can just barely be made to plane in the puffs—and then only when it's sailed at its best angle to the wind for planing. In such days, you may make your best time by sailing up in the puffs enough to get the boat planing (and then you may be able to sail downwind a bit more, holding the plane, since it's easier to sustain a plane than to start one), and sailing the compensating downwind direction when it's not blowing hard enough to plane.

As for the direction shifts when you're going downwind, the best thing to do is to forget it—except, of course, don't forget about retrimming your sails for the shifts. Beyond that, the direction shifts usually don't make enough difference to be worth fooling with.

Perhaps the single most important thing to say about helmsmanship is that it's a full-time job. It takes a special kind of concentration and determination to stay at it in a long race, making constant course and sail trim adjustments in response to continuing little changes in wind direction, wind strength, and waves—but that's what winners do. In a cruising class race, where you're sailing long distances, you shouldn't ask any one person to stay at the helm more than an hour or so at a time—he'd be bound to wear out. As I'll repeat in the last page of this book, winning is doing everything you know all of the time.

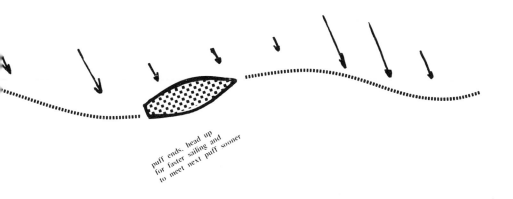

puff ends, head up for faster sailing and to meet next puff sooner

4

Key Racing Situations
A. Starting

Getting a good start is half the race in small, one-design class boats. After all, when the boats are very nearly equal (and yours should be) and all the skippers know how to sail, there isn't room for very much difference in how fast boats get around the course. The skipper who starts ahead has every shot at staying ahead, and the one who's behind will sail with dirty air, dirty water, and a dirty disposition for a long part of the race. The right way to win is to get a lead at the start and keep it. Catch-up sailing is the hard way.

You'll find lots of books on sailing tactics with long chapters about clever routines of sailing to and from the start line, all guaranteed to get you to the line at the best spot and at full speed. Trouble is, after you've perfected such a starting routine (actually, eleventeen of 'em to cover different winds, start line angles, and crowd situations), you'll find out that every race has something to goof it up. There always seems to be some dope charging along the line who doesn't know the rules, and gets in your way, or some poor soul in irons right where you want to go, or a change in wind at the last minute, or something else to wipe out your calculated start.

My advice is to forget about any kind of starting ritual. Instead, learn a few basic principles, and then play it by ear within those guidelines. The smaller the boats and the more crowded the line, the less hope you have of ever completing any kind of planned start.

You only need to start with three things right:

1. Be at the line on time—never early, and hopefully not more than two seconds late.
2. Hit the line moving as fast as you can—better a couple of seconds late and moving than on time and going slowly.
3. Go through the line in the clearest air hole you can find—better to be a little bit lonely, where you're not fighting backwind and wind blankets, than in a slightly

more "favored" position, and stuck in the middle of a crowd.

Starting on time. First you have to be sure that you know the starting signals that will be used for the race. No excuse not to: every race committee makes that completely public before the races get started. If you have any doubts at all, go around and ask.

> If committees use the customary system of guns and signal hoists where you race, never forget that the gun is unofficial, the signal hoist is the one that counts.

Next, you really have to have a watch of some kind, with a sweep second hand—even a five-dollar stopwatch if you can keep it running for five minutes. A very cheap watch will do, since almost anything will keep decent time for five minutes, and if it isn't waterproof, you can always wrap it in a plastic sandwich bag. If you sail with a crew aboard, make the crew responsible for keeping you advised of the time, and for counting down the last ten seconds or so. (Make him do it quietly—the guy in the next boat didn't read this book and doesn't know what time it is . . . why tell him?)

Third, you really have to know where the start line is. If you're right at one of the ends, that's no problem, but if you're not, don't kid yourself, you can't tell when you're there by looking right and left at the starting marks. The right way is to get a bearing while you're sailing around before the start. Line up the starting marks with whatever sticks out noticeably beyond them—beach landmarks, other buoys, anything you can spot in a hurry.

Finally you have to develop some skill at adjusting your timing. This amounts to getting a good feel for how to slow your boat down, and for how much time it takes to do some time-killing maneuvers.

> Think in terms of "little time-killers" and "big time-killers."
> Little time-killers, for getting rid of two or three seconds, or for dropping behind another boat, range from wiggling the boat in a series of tight little S-turns, through

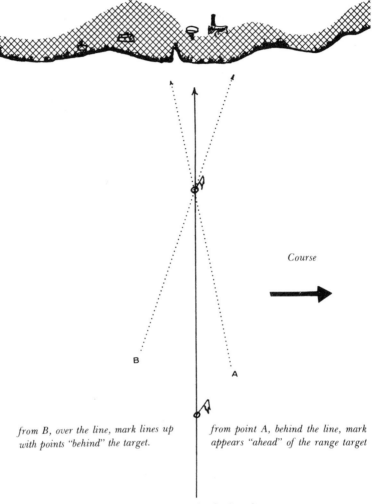

Course

from B, over the line, mark lines up with points "behind" the target.

from point A, behind the line, mark appears "ahead" of the range target

Before starting, sight the line from here to establish "range target" on shore line. (On water, use the compass bearing.)

luffing into the wind, to letting your sails flap. Experiment with these tricks until you get a feel for how much you can slow the boat down, how much room it takes to do it, and how much time and distance it takes to get moving again.

J slows by sailing a luffing course.
K makes delaying S-turns
L slacks sheets, luffing sails.

Big time-killers are primarily circling maneuvers, which include tacks or jibes, and get rid of ten seconds or so. They also take quite a bit of room. You can often use a circling maneuver to both get rid of 10 or 20 seconds and change by 30 or 40 feet where you're going to hit the line.

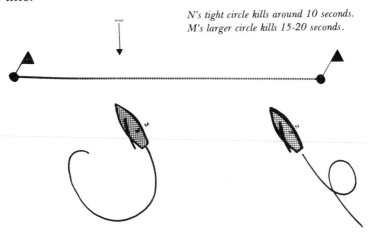

N's tight circle kills around 10 seconds.
M's larger circle kills 15-20 seconds.

Don't get too far away from the line; it's dangerous at any time before the start to be as far as 30 or 40 seconds' sailing from the line, and there's no need to go so far away. Even in the most crowded starting lines, there's always room enough to fool around five or ten lengths behind the line. In light airs, it's particularly important to stick around the line—nothing's more frustrating than to be becalmed or stuck in irons behind the line, while the rest of the fleet ghosts across five minutes ahead of you.

Never forget that the race committee has the only right time, as far as they're concerned. If their signal is late, and you go over early, too bad for you—your watch was the one that was wrong. So, until you've seen enough starts to be sure they'll be right, always leave yourself an extra one or two seconds . . . or an open pocket to leeward where you can cruise for a few feet at the line.

MAKE VERY SURE YOU UNDERSTAND THE RACING RULES THAT APPLY WHEN STARTING.

Starting at the favored end of the line. The normal starting line should be at right angles to the wind, and the first mark should be directly upwind from the line. In such a case, the trip to the first mark is exactly the same distance no matter where on the line you start.

Unfortunately, whether because of local traffic patterns and obstructions, or because of changes in the wind, or because of the race committee's carelessness, laziness, or funny ideas about breaking up crowds, something like half of all the starts you make will be on lines that are clearly not laid out at right angles to the wind.

In such a case, there's a measurable advantage to starting at one (the "favored") end of the line. Appendix E shows how to figure just how much advantage there is to the favored end—something you have to know in order to decide how much of a crowd you're willing to jostle with for room and air.

(On any off-the-wind start, whether downwind, reaching, or something that you can fetch close-hauled, there is a slight advantage in starting at the end that is closest to the mark, but it's much less important than other things. The other things that count more are finding clean air and room to maneuver, and if the mark is not far enough away to separate the fleet, it's important to start at the end of the line that will put you inside with buoy room when turning at the mark.)

Five basic starting tactics. There's a practical limit to preplanning starts, since so many things can change from one race to another—the length of the line, the angle of the line, the number of boats, the possibility of winds and currents favoring one side of the course, and so forth—but it helps to have a kit bag with several tricks in it from which you can choose and adapt as you go. Every racer's repertoire should include at least these:

1. the mainstay: a close-hauled drive to the line;
2. luffing into the windward corner;
3. approaching on port tack, and tacking near the line;
4. the dip-start; and
5. carving a hole for last-minute "barging."

All of these techniques will assume you're going to start on starboard tack—which you always will if it's possible to get across the line on starboard tack. Only village idiots and wild-eyed gamblers go near start lines on port tack except when port is the only way across. (Why: because starboard tack boats always have right-of-way over port tack boats at the start.)

1. The close-hauled drive to the line is the overall basic way of starting. The technique is, simply, to pre-plan your timing so that you know when and where to start getting up speed, then come steaming up to the line as close-hauled as the boat will sail fast, planning to hit the line right at the gun. The advantages of the technique are that it has you crossing the line going fast, and it has you approaching the line with reasonably good right-of-way. (Since you're close-hauled, only a luffing boat can threaten you with right-of-way from leeward, and you should be moving fast enough to easily evade any such luffing boats. You, on the other hand, will be right-of-way to leeward over most of the fleet, and hopefully can shout them out of your way.) The disadvantages are that you need to be very good at it to make the timing come out right, and that others have to cooperate some by not abusing your right-of-way. The system should work out very well for you when winds are reasonably reliable and when the line is not overcrowded. The most popular way to time such a start is like this:

Practice your timing until you know pretty closely how much time it takes to do a hairpin turn and get back up to full speed (probably around ten seconds). Hit the line going the wrong way at any chosen time (say two minutes to the gun) sailing a course that's just about opposite the close-hauled course you'll use for starting. Sail this way for half the time to the gun, less half the turn-around time—in this case, that would be one-minute- less- five-seconds = 55 seconds; then make your hairpin turn, and drive for the line.

This system should get you right to the line at the gun, going hard and fast—*if* the wind keeps steady, and if no one else gets in your way enough to affect your course or speed, and some other "if's" about your being consistent in your timing. (It has the special danger of taking you farther away from the line than is safe in anything other than very steady wind.)

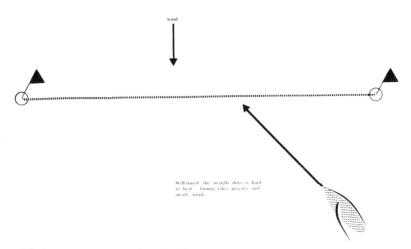

Well-timed, the straight drive is hard to beat. Timing takes practice and steady wind.

If the maneuver simply doesn't come out right when you practice it alone, you should be able to adjust the constant turn-around time (five seconds or whatever) that you subtract from the runaway course's time to sail.

2. Luffing into the windward corner is most effective in crowded starts and with decent wind, provided you have a light, fast-accelerating boat. The starting technique makes no sense at all in large, slow-starting boats.

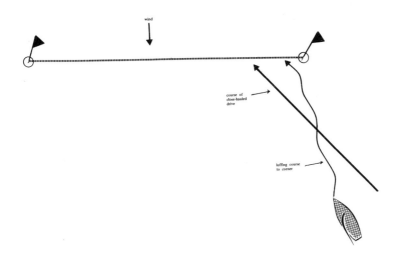

To use this system, you work yourself into a position about five boat lengths downwind from the line about ten seconds earlier than normal, then start working your boat up to windward, luffing as you go. By doing this, you become leeward right-of-way boat over anyone to windward of you, and by being early when you start the game, you should be ahead of everyone else who's approaching the line. You have a great deal of latitude about your timing, so with a little judgment and luck you should be able to mix luffing and full-bore sailing to keep you in front of everyone else, finally working yourself up toward the windward corner, about one length away at the point of time when you can make a final (speeding-up) dash for the line.

The main advantages of this technique are the almost impregnable right-of-way, which is very important in crowded starts, and the ability to make constant adjustments to your timing, which should get you to the line on the gun. The disadvantages are that you're not likely to cross the line at full speed, and that in either very light or very heavy winds you may have difficulty keeping the boat under control while half luffing. (In light winds, you risk losing steering way or going into irons, and in heavy winds if you let too much wind catch you, you'll soar across the line a mile early.)

When you use this start, you can go for any part of the line you like, but it's best at the starboard end where you can scrape the competition off on the mark. That way you protect your slow-moving boat from being blanketed by faster-moving boats that overtake to windward, and you should be in clear position to make a tack over onto port tack right after the start, getting away from leeward boats that would otherwise backwind you.

> If you're plagued by bargers in your club, this is the basic technique for teaching them better manners—luffing into the starboard corner closes bargers off like Superman stopping trains.
> (A "barger" is a boat without right-of-way trying to squeeze in at the mark from windward—or a boat reaching along the line so as to interfere with other right-of-way boats to leeward.)

3. Approaching on port tack, then tacking near the line is a great technique for once-in-a-while use. Try it a couple of times in a row and you'll find a hatchet man waiting to chop you off.

To make this start, you simply come at the left end of the line barreling along on port tack. Your whole area should be clear of traffic until you're within the last half-dozen lengths of the line, since everyone else is coming in from the other side of the course on starboard tack. You figure to keep coming until the crowd begins to get thick, with considerable freedom to sail nearly parallel with the line and about three lengths downwind of it; then, when the timing looks right, you simply tack onto starboard tack to leeward of the nearest competitors, and off you go with a well-timed start and a safe-leeward position. (That is, leeward boat with right-of-way and so positioned that you're ahead of the windward boat's wind blanket, while your backwind damages his performance—see page 68).

The port tack approach usually works out well on thinly populated starting lines, and allows you to do a top-notch job on timing. In very crowded starts, or any start in which the port end of the line is favored, it's suicide—you'll surely find such a cloud of starboard tackers that you can't get anywhere near the line before you're forced to tack onto

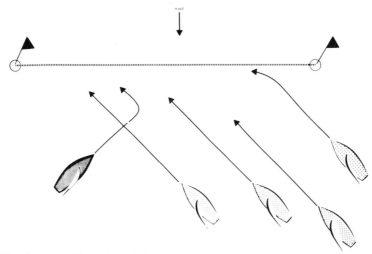

The black boat can pick its place if there's open room, but has to give right-of-way until the tack has been completed.

starboard for self-preservation. (In drifting airs, when there's a chance of not being able to tack on short notice, forget it.) Obviously, if the starboard end of the line is significantly favored, this is no start for you—there's no way to get a port tack boat past the left half of the line without having to duck the whole fleet.

4. The dip-start is gamblers' paradise on long lines; on short lines, you can only get away with it when there are very few boats or when starboard tack boats can barely fetch the line (because of the wind angle). It's always dangerous, since you're coming at the line with no right-of-way.

To dip-start, you approach the line from the windward side, reaching toward the line as fast as you can go, and planning to cross over onto the starting side of the line just before the gun, then make a little buttonhook turn to start properly. If you get in the way of any boat to leeward of you, you will be barging, of course, but the idea is that you should be able to pick a hole in the line where you can get away with it. When the line is long, most of the boats in the middle won't be sure where it is, so they'll be late and should leave a hole big enough for you. If they don't, you're in very big trouble.

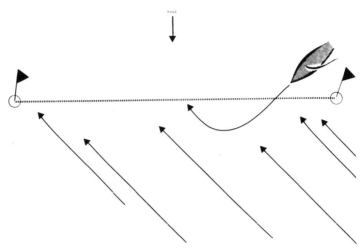

Black's dip-start can work, given plenty of room on the line, some late boats in the middle, lots of luck.

The advantages of the dip-start are that it has you approaching the line sailing alone and downwind, so you should have free room to maneuver and thus get perfect timing, and it has you approaching in clean fresh air while others in a crowded start are fighting backwind, wake, wind shadows, and each other—so you may get away sailing faster than the competition. The disadvantage is that you're a sitting duck for any leeward boat (and the whole fleet will be leeward of you), and if you can't find a hole you'll be stuck over the line when the gun goes off. (By the way, there's a special starting rule that applies on re-starts after general recalls, which disallows the dip-start—and some clubs apply that rule all of the time, so you can't use it at all where they do.)

5. Carving yourself a hole for a little last-minute barging is a sort of middle-of-the-line variation of the "luffing into the windward corner" technique. In this start, what you do is approach the line a little early, luffing very closely to head-to-wind as you get within the last couple of boat lengths of the line. By doing this, you leave a sort of hole of empty water to leeward of yourself (while maintaining a very safe right-of-way) which should get to be as big as one to two boat-lengths wide. Then, at the last moment just as you approach the line, you fall off into this hole, gathering speed as you go, wheeling over the line right at the gun.

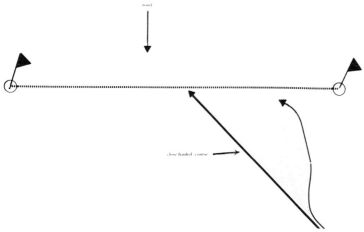

It is relatively difficult for competitors to enter the shaded area . . . this becomes the "carved-out hole" in which last moment timing adjustments may be sailed as well as an accelerating dive.

The advantage of the technique is primarily its safety (since you are luffing, no leeward boats can get near you) and its handiness for adjusting your timing all the way to the gun. The disadvantage is that unless you get lucky, there really won't be quite enough room to get up to full speed at the gun, so others will be moving fast enough to sail past you after the gun. It's a reasonably safe way of making better-than-average starts.

B. Turning marks of the course

Good technique at the marks counts two ways. First, places change quickly at marks, and the better skippers ordinarily move up a place or two when marks are crowded—and, it figures, novices are apt to move down a place or two. Second, about half of the foul-outs occur around marks (most of the rest are at the starts).

The basic principles for good marksmanship are:

1. Keep the boat moving fast around the turn.
2. Get the inside position if you possibly can.
3. Protect yourself against being luffed as you come away from the mark.

The problems you have to face at the marks are quite different between "windward" marks (ones you have to tack to get to, or ones where you have to tack to make the turn) and "leeward" marks (that's all the others, of course). Therefore, we'll discuss them separately.

Windward marks. The basic rules of starboard tack *vs.* port tack apply at windward marks, and the rights to "buoy room" apply only to boats on the same tack at such marks. Therefore, if you're not all alone, you *must* arrive at the mark on starboard tack.

You can hear a lot of fancy talk about the right ways to approach windward marks, but what it boils down to is:

1. If you make the final (starboard) tack to the buoy a long one, there's considerable exposure to over- or under-standing the mark, and either one hurts.

If you over-stand, you've wasted some sailing distance, and worse, there's a good chance that others will tack into a leeward overlap, beating you to the inside berth.

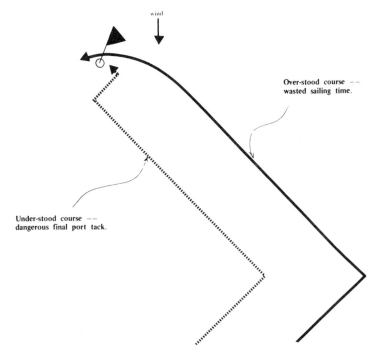

wind

Over-stood course — — wasted sailing time.

Under-stood course — — dangerous final port tack.

If you under-stand, then you're stuck with having to make a little last-minute extra port tack, which costs you extra tacking right when you don't want it, and puts you in the no-right-of-way spot just when it hurts the most. 2. Since the 1969 rules, it's been certified as clean and fair to tack into an inside overlap, rating buoy room, closer than two lengths from the mark. This makes it very attractive to come in toward the mark on your last long tack on port tack, then swing over onto starboard tack anywhere between, say, one and three or four lengths from the mark—making that last distance to the mark on starboard tack.

This business of tacking into overlap fairly close to the buoy gets very attractive except when there is a large, close-packed bunch of boats approaching the mark. You can get a pretty good feel for how crowded it's going to be at the mark something like halfway there. Start planning early. If it is going to be crowded when you arrive, then plan on a fairly long final starboard tack, and do the best you can about working into an inside berth.

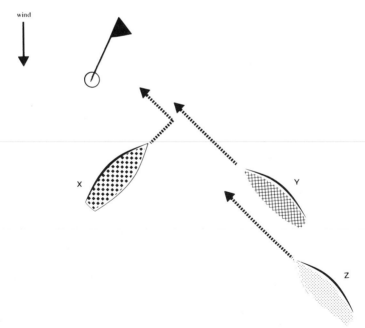

X may tack into overlap and claim room . . . if he can find room to approach and tack.

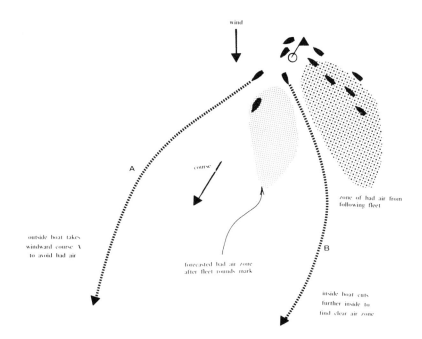

wind

course

A

outside boat takes
windward course \
to avoid bad air

forecasted bad air zone
after fleet rounds mark

zone of bad air from
following fleet

B

inside boat cuts
further inside to
find clear air zone

If it isn't going to be really thick when you get there, then figure on the port tack near-approach, with a short final starboard tack, and you have an excellent chance of pulling the inside berth. (All the troops who learned under the old rules are stuck with the habit of making long final starboard tack approaches, and they tend to be sitting ducks for the boat that tacks to leeward.) Do make sure you study the rules, though, and don't tack too close to other boats, nor too close for others to have a fair chance to give you your buoy room.

As you come out of the turn at a windward mark, your big effort should be on keeping clear wind in your sails. Most often you'll be going downwind from the mark, and all the boats turning behind you will pour wind blanket at you—so you have to come out of the turn at an angle away from the mark to find clear air. Now that you know what you have to do, the answer is obvious—if you're outside, swing on wide so you'll be to windward of following boats on the outside of the course; if you're inside, sail in a bit extra to get away from being dead downwind of the mark.

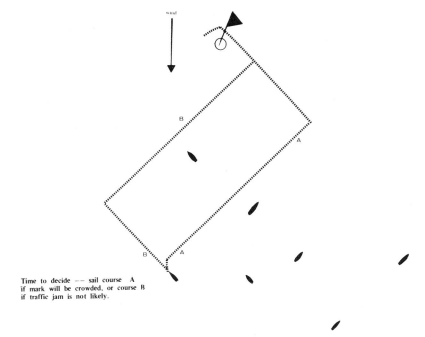

Time to decide — — sail course A
if mark will be crowded, or course B
if traffic jam is not likely.

Leeward marks. Working the turns at leeward marks is considerably tougher than at the windward marks for two reasons. First, you have considerably more maneuverability when sailing off the wind, so there are more things you can get away with, which gives you more choices on strategy. Second, port tack boats rank equally with starboard tack boats when claiming buoy room, which considerably increases the number of boats you have to worry about.

If you're not really sure of the rules about buoy room, you really ought to bone up on them before getting very involved at leeward marks. To oversimplify:

- Boats overlapped on the inside at the point where the nearer boat is two lengths away from the leeward marks rate room, irrespective of which tack they are on.
- Buoy room includes room to jibe.
- Leading boats (clear ahead) rate room to jibe, and following boats must keep clear.
- If a jibe is natural to the course, then a prompt jibe is compulsory when overlapped.

• Buoy room rights end as soon as the inside boat no longer overlaps the mark, at which point an outside boat could have the right to luff sharply.

The basic principles to shoot for at leeward marks are:

1. Always try for the inside berth with buoy room.
2. It's better to be close astern than outside, particularly if the next leg is a beat.
3. A smooth turn that doesn't slow the boat is preferable to a sharp buttonhook, even though the sharp turn may leave you a bit farther upwind.

About half the boats you'll race against don't understand the problems in smooth steering, so they'll sucker for the usual problem of bad helmsmanship—they'll approach the mark as close as they can, then swing sharply as they pass abeam of it. This will cause them both to turn too sharply, killing their speed, and to make a turn which leaves them sagging off to leeward of the mark by two or more boat widths. You, on the other hand, know that the better maneuver is to approach the mark a bit wide and steer so that you're close aboard the mark as you *leave it,* which leaves you in the windward berth going away from the mark, where it counts.

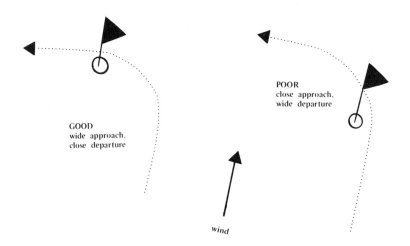

GOOD
wide approach.
close departure

POOR
close approach.
wide departure

wind

Three basic maneuvers at the mark should be instinctive to you.

One, protect your position when you have the inside berth coming up to the mark.

Two, steal the weather berth leaving the mark, when you can't get the inside slot, by cutting behind the insider who swings too wide (at your own risk, of course).

Three, luff the insider when you're stuck with the outside berth, just as soon as he clears the mark.

Let's look at these in turn.

When you have the inside overlap to rate buoy room, your job is to protect that position throughout the rounding maneuver and immediately afterward. If, as you're approaching the mark, your nearest competitor is following and threatening to overtake on the inside, you should try to force him outside by sailing sharply toward the inside yourself. Then, once you're inside the two-lengths distance (at which point it's too late for him to claim buoy room), you swing into enough of a curve to make a smooth turn at the mark.

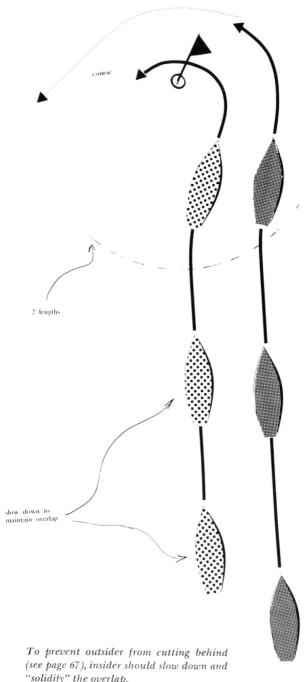

course

2 lengths

slow down to
maintain overlap

*To prevent outsider from cutting behind
(see page 67), insider should slow down and
"solidify" the overlap.*

If, instead, your nearest competitor is on the outside, but somewhat trailing, you may be wisest deliberately to slow down just a little bit, enough to assure that he *stays stuck* outside as you go around the mark.

When you're on the outside, you can play it safe and stick to the outside, hoping to throw a luff at the insider as he completes passing the mark, or you can gamble on finding room to slip inside from behind as he rounds. Don't try that gamble if there are any other boats near behind the two of you, or you'll end up losing a tangle about rights-of-way for sure. When there aren't others too close, however, consider the possibility of slowing down a bit and swinging a bit wide just before you get to the mark, then finding room close to the mark and astern of the insider. If you know more about making smooth turns than he does, and especially if there's a jibe at the mark, you may be able to grab the windward berth as you leave the buoy—with or without slipping in between the other boat and the mark. Remember, this is an at-your-own-risk gamble, with no right-of-way, so don't sneak inside until you're *sure* there's enough room.

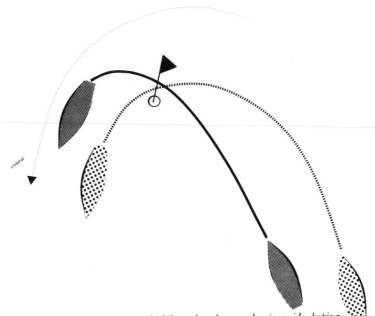

Approaching on the outside, it's sometimes worthwhile to slow down and swing wide, hoping for room to cut inside. (It requires that the insider makes a poor approach and rounding.)

C. Mid-course situations

Whether you're trying to pass another boat, or defend against one that's passing you, or are simply about to cross-tack another that's on the opposite tack, it's essential that you have a feel for the ways in which one boat influences the speed of another. The two important influences are known as "backwind" and "wind blanket" (or "shadow"). Another item, a lot less important in small boats than big boats, is wake.

Backwind. Backwind is the dirty air that is sent off to wind-ward and astern of boats, especially close-hauled boats. It's very important at close range.

> Remind yourself that the drive of a close-hauled sail is the result of developing low pressure on the leeward side of the sail, compared to high pressure on the windward side of the sail. This is the result of air on the leeward side having to pass along the convex side of the sail, which is a longer trip than the straight line air can follow on the windward side; to make the longer distance, the air must flow a little faster, and *pressure is less where velocity is greater.*

Now then, the boat to windward of you is trying to develop its low pressure area near to the same point in the air where your boat is developing its high pressure area. The result is, your backwind (high pressure) ruins his efficiency—and he ends up going slower. To top this, the air flow off your sail is "bent" enough to change the relative direction of the wind his sails get, and the result of that is that he won't be able to point as high to the wind without luffing as if you weren't there.

Boats close aboard to windward, then, soon find that they can't keep up with the leeward competitors, and they can't point as high, so they either have to tack away from the leeward boat, or else will end up falling behind and into the turbulent air astern of the boat that was to leeward.

More so-called backwind lies astern, as the result of the air turbulence being dumped by the used-up air that's been past your sails—and this turbulence will cause the following boat to go slower, and still find itself not pointing as high as the leading boat.

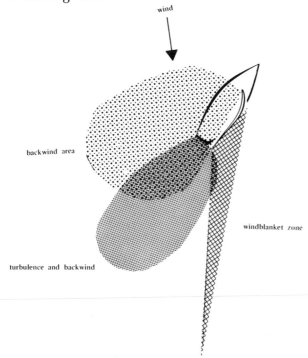

Backwind is so important that for fifty years or so people have been referring to the area of backwind as the "hopeless position"—and that it is. You have to be very much better than your competitor to sail successfully through his backwind. As you would expect, the backwind effects decrease as boats get farther apart, but they are noticeable for up to two or three mast-lengths, and are very important within one mast-length.

THE SAFE LEEWARD POSITION

Analysis of the angle and strength of airstreams shows two things happening: (1) the air-stream is bent; (2) the airstream is slowed to windward and astern, while it is accelerated to leeward and ahead. The shaded area to leeward of the sails in this illustration shows a zone in which air is moving 10% or more faster than the average wind, while the darker shading to windward of the sails shows the area of air moving 10% or more slower than the average wind.

In position A, an opponent would get some favorable wind shift ("lift") but weaker wind — he may be able to pinch up and get away from the leeward boat.

In position B, an opponent is hopeless, getting both a "heading" wind shift and slower wind — he must tack away, or expect to fall astern and to leeward.

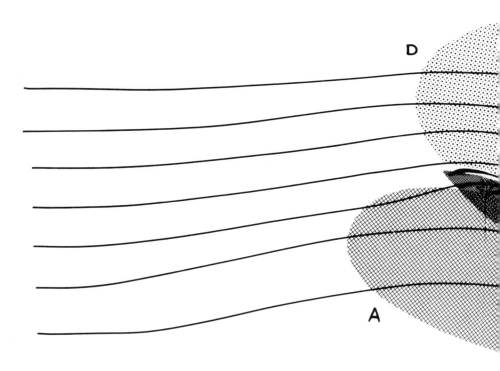

True
Wind

In position C an opponent gets "headed" by an unfavorable wind angle, but may be able to hang on owing to the stronger wind — he should fall off the wind a bit, hoping to accelerate and get up to position D.

Position D is the safe leeward *— here, one gets both a favorable "lifting" wind angle and faster air.*

The bending of wind in the vicinity of sails has been generally understood for many years; the above illustration is based upon recent studies by Mr. Arvel Gentry (first published in SAIL *magazine) which have recently added an understanding of the changes in wind velocity . . . showing how jib and mainsail affect one another, and showing the effects of nearby boats upon one another.*

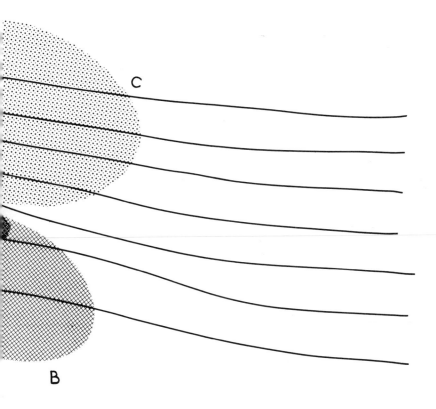

Being close aboard to windward is deathly on close-hauled courses, where backwind is significant. As the course "frees"—becomes less close to the wind—backwind becomes less important. It's still noticeable on beam reaches (wind directly on the side), and dwindles away quickly to the point of nothing on courses that are mostly with the wind.

On close-to-the-wind courses, therefore, windward should do all that's possible to avoid ever being within a length or two of any leeward boat that is forward of abeam. On a beat, windward should usually tack away. On close reaches, the windward boat should immediately pinch farther up to windward to get away.

Wind blanket. This term needs little explanation; it is simply the area downwind of your sail which is sheltered from the full strength of the wind by the "shadow" or hole in the wind caused by your sail. As with backwind, the farther apart the boats are, the less noticeable the effect. Wind blanket is killing within half a mast-length or so, and very hard to notice farther away than two-and-a-half or three mast-lengths. Chasing boats downwind you have to *aim* the wind blanket. Remember that it goes out in the direction your wind pennant points (or would point if in clear, nonturbulent air)—that is, the direction of the apparent wind, after considering your boat's course and speed. Aim for your opponent's best sail—the spinnaker if he has one flying, otherwise the main.

Wake and turbulence left by modern racing boats are very small, yet have a noticeable effect on other boats in light airs or fairly smooth water. In heavy winds, when the boats are moving near top speed, or in choppy water full of roughness anyway, the effects are so small that you can spend your time worrying about something else. It does help to know what to look for on those special occasions (like a close finish) where a foot one way or the other can really count. There are three wakes to look for: bow wave, quarter wave, and following stern waves. (Your boat, sailed properly with the transom out of the water, won't make much quarter or stern wake; once in a rare while you'll find smooth enough water to practice trimming your boat by experimenting with finding the place for your weight that produces the absolute minimum wake—the less wake, the better trim.)

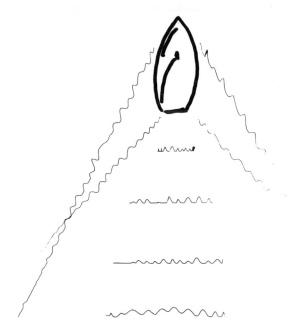

Going downwind in light air and smooth water, you may find you can just about pass an opponent, but can't quite get across his quarter wave. The theoretical place to pass is at the point where his bow and quarter waves cross. Here, the two waves should cancel each other, offering a point where your boat can pass without having to climb up over a wave. (On close-hauled courses, backwind and wind blanket are so much more important that you can forget about the wakes.)

Crossing tacks. Beating to windward, boats frequently meet on opposite tacks. The port tack skipper, if he can't cross safely ahead of the right-of-way starboard tacker, must decide whether to tack onto starboard before reaching the path of the starboard tacker, or whether to bear off and pass astern.

You should know that passing astern doesn't cost much lost time or distance. For a rule of thumb, if your (port tack) course would cross starboard's course ahead of midships, sailing behind starboard will cost about one-half length's sailing; if your course would cross aft of midships, sailing behind will cost practically nothing.

This is because you sail a little faster while bearing off to pass astern, and then when passing through starboard's backwind area you pick up a momentary lift —which wouldn't do a big boat any good, but is enough for an alert small-boat skipper to luff up, recovering nearly all the windward distance he lost while steering to pass astern.

As an alternative to bearing off and passing astern, port tack may decide to tack to leeward of starboard. If he does so in such a way as to end up on a parallel course and at least a little bit ahead of even, he will have starboard backwinded and should move out ahead.

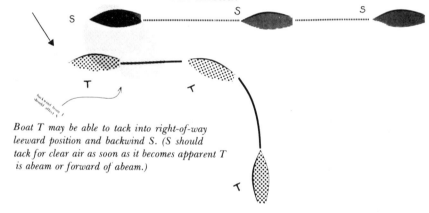

Boat T may be able to tack into right-of-way leeward position and backwind S. (S should tack for clear air as soon as it becomes apparent T is abeam or forward of abeam.)

If port (now leeward) pulls off the tack smoothly and winds up moving well and a bit ahead of starboard, the backwind should, within a couple of minutes' sailing, dump starboard into the hopeless position.

This will work for port, if he's good at tacking, in most cases where his course would just about cross starboard's bow. When you're tacking well, the tack-and-recover-speed maneuver costs between one half and one boat length—and you have to end up as leeward around one quarter length or more ahead to dish out a heavy dose of backwind.

If port pulls it off, starboard has to tack to get out of the backwind.
Port has to be careful not to tack too close—a foul.

5

Tactics

There is simply no end to tactical possibilities in small boat racing—which is what makes the sport. The challenge of coming up with effective tactical maneuvers at the right time is what makes it a truly great game—and one that requires quick decisions, skill, and some gambling impulses.

In this section, we'll try to equip you with a feel for how to skipper some of the basic tactical maneuvers. As to when and where you try them, well, that's what makes it your own race.

Practically all of the tactical ploys are some one or other—or combination of—these maneuvers:

Luffing
Covering
Avoiding cover
Passing
Wind-hunting and splitting tacks
Playing wind slants and currents

Luffing

Before getting into this section, if you're not already familiar with the rules about luffing rights, you should turn to pages 5, 166. Generally you have luffing rights (after starting) if you're to leeward, and have never been (during the life of the overlap) far enough back of windward for his helmsman to be abeam your mast.

Luffing consists of making an alteration of course toward the wind, up to and including head-to-wind if you like. After starting, when you have luffing rights, you may make such a maneuver as sharply as you like and without warning. You may luff with the hopes of hitting your opponent (or all but hitting him and then curtailing the luff, which is the same as if you hit him), and if you succeed, he's fouled out. You may also luff your opponent with the purpose of making him move over to windward, either to obtain for yourself a better position at a mark, or to make room for you to sail in a direction that you prefer. Finally, a good luffing maneuver can often chop off a boat that's passing you, tucking him back behind where you want him.

Luffing-to-kill a boat to windward, which is legal, is available to you when the opponent tries to pass you close aboard to windward. In a small boat, which maneuvers very sharply when you want, an opponent that's to windward and not farther than a boat width or so upwind is a sitting duck. All you have to do is swing sharply to windward, and you'll hit him before he has a chance to know what's happening. Moral—don't you try to pass close aboard to windward—it's pure suicide!

A sharp, sudden luff almost can't miss a nearby windward boat ... windward is fouled out (note: fast luffing is not legal before starting).

When you set out to luff a boat passing to windward, you better luff hard and fast, or you're bound to end up farther behind.

There are several different situations in which skippers put their boats in peril of being luffed out of the race. One, the stupidest, is the simple case of a boat trying to pass another to windward; leeward swings up to tag him, and that's it. The next most common, not so stupid as unthinking, is the skipper with the inside berth rounding a mark, who will be windward boat as the rounding maneuver is completed. Thinking himself safe at the mark, under the protection (which he is) of the buoy room rules, the inside-and-windward skipper forgets that his buoy room protection ends as soon as his boat no longer overlaps the mark; turn the mark, clear it, and surprise surprise, leeward is luffing and the inside boat is dead.

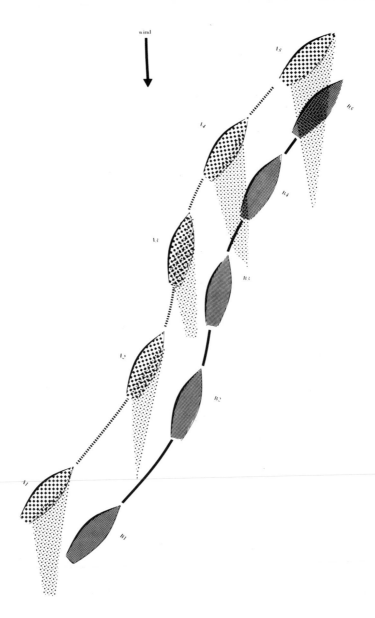

Slow-and-easy luff puts windward ahead (sailing the shorter course on the inside of the turn). The leeward boat ends up in windward's windblanket and falls behind.

No longer overlapping the mark, "buoy room" rights are ended; leeward luffs.

Other ways in which windward may find himself ready to die include cases where boats running downwind all jibe at once, because of a windshift (say), or where the boats were near each other as they crossed the starting line (new overlaps, for the purpose of luffing rights, begin when boats clear the start line), or any other way in which a new overlap is established, creating a newly leeward boat with luffing rights. And remember, when one boat tacks into a leeward overlap, he has luffing rights as soon as the tack is completed.

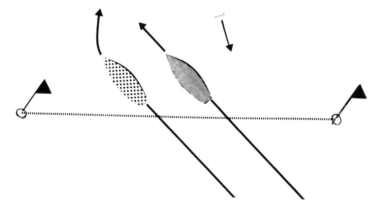

Both boats have completely cleared the start line — leeward may luff immediately.

Luffing an opponent in order to sail him over to windward might be in order, for example, if you think you can edge him into some dirty air that he'll get and you won't (say the lee of an island). Another occasion would be to cause him to blanket a downwind and leading opponent. A third case might be just to get yourself into some clear air—he'll get it with you, but you have to move him in order to enjoy it yourself.

Luffing an opponent in order to break up a passing maneuver before it goes too far, and to protect yourself from his wind blanket, is one of the most common luffing maneuvers. On this one, much like the luffing-to-kill, it's best to luff fairly hard and sharply if you're going to do it at all. If you go slow and easy, the following boat usually makes better time and distance than you do, and he wins. Besides, you want him to get the idea that he can't win going to windward of you and *give up the idea* before both of you go wandering all over the course, which is a game that doesn't help either one of you, but brings joy to the hearts of all the other boats that are following you.

Covering

"Covering" an opponent refers to all the clean and dirty things you do to stay ahead of an opponent; mostly, you cover opponents one at a time, but the really foxy skippers try to strategize things so that they can cause the nearest several opponents to stick together, where they can cover them all at once.

On the wind (beating), the basic rule to covering is to stay near to, and on the same tack as, the opponent you're covering. The whole idea is to guarantee that he can't get a little puff, or favorable windshift that you don't also get—first. Additionally, when things work out right, you'll dish him wind blanket or wake that will make him fall farther behind. When you're substantially ahead, cover by always staying between your opponent and the next mark, preferably on the same tack and preferably more or less directly upwind of him.

When you're ahead by a good bit and rounding a leeward mark, the standard procedure is to sail on one tack for half the distance by which you lead the opponent, then on the

With an opponent at P (say 10 lengths behind) when you reach the mark Q, sail so as to be directly upwind of Q when opponent reaches it (by sailing on each tack half the amount of the lead . . . measured in time, not distance, as opponent may be planing much faster than you sail). Then cover by sailing on whichever tack opponent chooses after rounding the mark.

other tack until he gets to the mark. This should put you dead upwind of him when he rounds, after which you go onto whichever tack he chooses after rounding. See Appendix D for details on optimal covering positions.

Running downwind, the standard procedure for covering is to stay as much as possible in front of your opponent (but just enough to windward to assure that he won't wind-blanket you.) Thus, if he goes chasing off to the left side of the course, you chase off to the same side, staying between him and the next mark. That way, if he should get a nice special puff of wind, you'll get it too; if he finds a course that will get him planing, you will too; if he gets going and catches up, you'll be in a position to luff him.

P luffs up to pass Q to windward; Q responds by luffing (in order to avoid threat of windblanket and to stay in front).

Avoiding cover

On the wind (beating) the standard technique for getting out from under a covering boat is to *split tacks*; that is, as soon as the leading boat gets on the same tack you're on, you tack. If he's really out to cover you, he'll tack as soon as he sees you've tacked—so you tack again. This gets to be what's called a "tacking duel", and there are two ways you can win at it. One, if you've practiced more than he has, you'll tack a bit more efficiently than he does, so you should make a few feet on every tack; make enough tacks, and you'll keep catching up until at some point you're even, your starboard tack will catch him on port tack, and you're ahead.

The other way you may win at this game is that you, the covered boat, get to choose when you're going to tack —he cannot choose, but is forced to go immediately after he sees you tacking. This is an advantage for you because you get to set yourself (and your crew) for each tack, whereas your covering opponent is in a hurry, so your tacks ought to average being smoother and faster.

Perhaps more importantly, if there are the usual little puffs and windshifts, you will more than half the time be able to pick a moment to tack that's favorable for you, with a little shift making the tack attractive at the time you choose . . . whereas, since you're choosing the moment to tack, the timing often will be wrong for your opponent.

When the tacking duel really gets hot and heavy, try a fake tack—start a tack, and then when you see that your opponent has started his covering tack, interrupt your tack at about the point where you're head to wind, going back onto the tack you were on. This is supposed to leave your opponent stuck on opposite tacks from you, because when he catches on, he'll just be coming out of one tack, and moving too slowly to tack again without risking going into irons.

Off the wind, avoiding cover is tougher, but fortunately it isn't so urgent as when you're on the wind. The following boat, when both boats are going downwind, is in a fine position to attack (by blanketing). Indeed, the following boat's problem, if it's close enough to blanket, is picking the right time.

The point at which to blanket and pass is just before reaching the next mark. Pass too soon, and the other

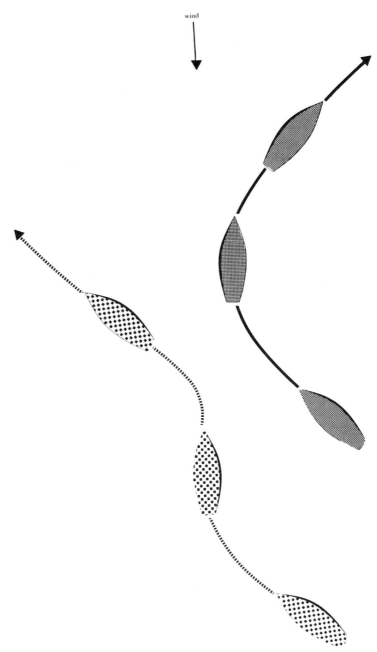

Fake tack can leave the covering boat without enough speed to risk an immediate second tack, thus achieving split tack to break cover.

skipper has a chance to blanket right back; too late, and you won't have time to get inside at the mark. About two boat-lengths for each knot of speed is the right place to start blanketing—say ten lengths away from the mark in a typical centerboarder.

Passing

It ain't easy. While you're out to pass the boat next ahead, you can bet your Topsiders he's out to keep you from doing it. It helps to know how your chances are best, and you have to be sure to avoid getting into a tangle about rights-of-way. That's what this section is about. The chances, and the right approaches, are quite different with boats that are close-hauled than with boats that are running free. (Close-hauled, it's usually better to just go about your business, maxi-tacking as described in Appendix D.)

Passing on the wind—close-hauled or nearly so—you can almost never get by really close aboard the boat ahead. You don't dare try to pass close to windward (which is next to impossible in steady winds, anyway, owing to the backwind effect), because you put yourself in position to be killed by a sharp luff from the other boat. Passing close to leeward is about as hard because of the problems in getting through the other boat's wind blanket. In either case—to windward or to leeward—you want to pass at least a boat length away from your opponent.

Passing to windward, beating, you have to start working your way well upwind of your opponent, starting from more than a boat length behind (to keep out of his backwind zone). If he's sailing as well as you are, you won't make it. You have to be sharper about luffing up a bit on each of the little lifts and puffs that comes along, and you have to be a bit sharper about keeping your boat from heeling quite as much as his in the puffs. You have to trim perfectly, and stay smooth on the steering.

If everything works out right, over the course of two minutes' sailing or so, you'll be able to work up into a position that's a boat length or more to windward, and a touch ahead or at least abeam. If you can get to this point, you

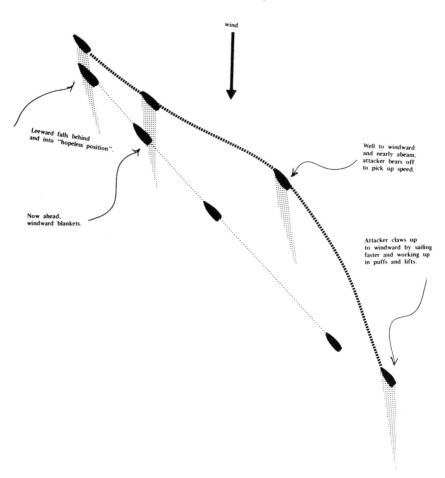

wind

Leeward falls behind
and into "hopeless position".

Now ahead,
windward blankets.

Well to windward
and nearly abeam,
attacker bears off
to pick up speed.

Attacker claws up
to windward by sailing
faster and working up
in puffs and lifts.

should be able to pass by easing off onto a very slightly
more leeward course, get your boat going a bit faster, and
slide down to a position that is enough ahead to wind-
blanket your opponent. Throughout the maneuver, you
must be alert to defend against a luffing attack from your
opponent.

If he luffs, you must respond instantly but smoothly,
turning just a little slower than he does, using the distance that you so carefully kept between your boats to
slide a bit ahead and hit him with your wind blanket as
you both come back to course from the luff.

   Once ahead, try to stay just a bit to windward and sheet in your sails as tight as you can without ruining their set—this increases the backwind effect and helps to keep him behind you.

Passing to leeward, beating, you have to steer a course that is far enough to leeward of your opponent to avoid his backwind and wind-blanket zones. This means at least a full boat-length to leeward. Bear off a bit to pick up some extra speed—hopefully just when a bit of extra strong wind hits you, as it has more effect on boats sailing not quite so close to the wind—and try to drive through your opponent's wind-blanket zone. If you do get through, then sail parallel and to leeward until you're abeam or forward. At this point, you're in position to backwind, and you start pinching and luffing on puffs to get back as close aboard him as you can. (You now have right-of-way, as leeward boat, but do not have luffing rights, so the windward boat has the obligation to keep clear of you; you have an obligation to sail no higher than a proper course—which means close-hauled when beating.) Exaggerate the backwind effect as much as you can by sheeting sails as flat as they'll go without killing the boat—you should then pull clear ahead, putting your opponent into the "hopeless position" in your backwind astern.

At position 1 the attacker (A) bears off to gain speed, then plunges through the windblanket at 2. Beginning at 3, the attacker pinches and luffs at every puff to backwind at 4, 5, whereafter he should pull clear ahead.

   Passing on downwind legs, you're in much better shape. Your opponent's backwind isn't effective, and you should be in position to hit him with your wind blanket. Actually, when boats are close and running downwind, one of your bigger problems is deciding *when* to pass him. It's important to remember that running dead before the wind is a boat's slowest point of sailing; reaching a bit across the wind is enough faster to make up for the extra distance traveled. Therefore, when attacking a boat that's ahead, you can afford to do quite a bit of dodging back and forth behind him, maneuvering to hit him with wind blanket, without losing much if any distance.

Generally, unless you're nearing a mark of the course so that you have to pass to leeward in order to get the inside slot at the mark, the right way is to pass to windward. When you do, remember to leave plenty of room between boats to protect against being luffed.

Passing to windward, running downwind, your wind blanket will slow your opponent at some point, letting you surge past. Sail a boat length or more to windward, to leave margin enough to avoid a luff, then concentrate on hitting his best sail with your wind blanket. When you hit him, he'll slow down very appreciably, and as you pull ahead enough to call "mast abeam," ending his luffing rights, you can fall off onto a parallel course until you're clear ahead. Then you can fall off even more, to your

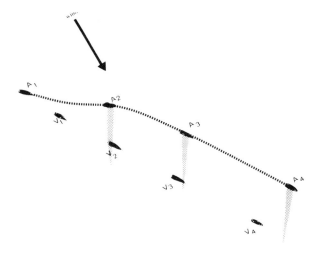

At position 1, attacker (A) luffs windward of victim (V), catching V with windblanket at position 2; thereafter, moving faster, A pulls clear ahead.

proper course to the next mark. From there on, you're only worried about having your opponent do the same thing back at you.

Passing to leeward, running, you have to pass far enough to leeward to stay clear of your opponent's wind blanket, then after you're clear ahead, reach (reaching is faster sailing than is running) up through the wind blanket—picking a point that is far enough away from your opponent so that the wind blanket is quite narrow, (about two lengths), and picking a course that is fast enough so that you won't be blanketed more than a second or two.

Since your opponent isn't likely to be completely asleep, you'll often find it advantageous to make a feint to one side, then pass on the other side. Remember that the boat ahead can always luff up to windward, but is not allowed to bear off below a proper course in order to interfere with you when you're maneuvering to pass to leeward. Don't hesitate to hail your opponent if he appears to be bearing off below a proper course—lots of skippers aren't clear about their obligations not to do so, so tell them.

Beginning at position 1, the attacker (A) bears off to leeward. At 2 he hardens up and reaches through the end of the windblanket. After 3 his sail is through the windblanket and, in clear air, he pulls ahead.

Wind hunts and split tacks

On a beating leg of the course, when you're behind, the right thing to do is usually to go someplace different from the boat ahead of you. On average, if you go anywhere near the same way the leader goes, you have nothing to do but follow him. The basic principle is to try for some luck—look for a chance to get a favorable bit of wind that he doesn't get.

The basic technique is to split tacks—if the leader is sailing on starboard tack, which goes toward the left side of the course, then you go over to the right side of the course on port tack. Doing so will at least get you out of his wake and dirty air, and gives you a chance for getting something lucky that he doesn't get.

Deciding whether or not to do this requires some weighing of risks. If you're in fairly decent position, in the front part of the fleet, you may decide that the right thing to do is to try to stay in front of the boats that are now behind you, in which case you cover the following fleet as best you can, letting the fellow in front of you win or lose, however it works out.

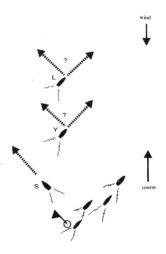

In position Y you must choose between covering the fleet on port tack, or splitting from the leader (L) by tacking. If you tack, L will face the same decision.

On the other hand, if it's more important to you to try to beat the fellows in front—and certainly if you're way down in the pack—then you might as well take a chance. Chance is what it is; odds are, the fellow in front is going to be going to the side of the course that appears most likely to be good, except that his decision will be influenced by his desire to cover the boats behind him. What you do, when you split tacks, is put a squeeze on him—if you go way off to one side of the course, he has to choose between covering you and covering the majority of the pack (even when he believes your course is likely to be a good one). Unless you're the only boat he has to beat, his choice is obvious: he has to cover the fleet. That leaves you free to hunt around for some part of the pond where the wind may be a bit stronger, or on a better slant.

Sail on the split tack as far away from the leader as you can; look for good wind slants and currents, and hope that the leader gets busy with nearby boats, leaving you to sail as fast as you know how in undisturbed wind and water.

Wind slants and currents

The name of the game is to look for better places to sail. The wind is different on different parts of the water, and so are the currents, whether from tides or from a river's flow. The basics that apply:

Wind is strongest near the shore when it's caused by thermal convection (the summer-afternoon onshore breeze, for example).

Wind is dirtied up and weakened by shoreline obstructions, like trees, cliffs, and large buildings.

Wind changes direction a bit at shorelines, bending to cross the shore at closer to right angles.

Water currents are stronger in deep water, milder in shallow water, and there will be "backwater" or eddies at obstructions.

In addition, for reasons that escape me, you'll find lanes or streaks of better wind out in open water. These are often visible from quite a distance away—dark color on relatively calm water, or obvious bunches of spray and whitecaps on windier days. Sometimes these lanes hang on for plenty long enough to go over and get into them. When one boat's in one, and the others aren't, it can change a race. Keep an eye out for 'em.

Chasing for *thermals at the shoreline* is so simple there isn't much more to say about it. Look for them on hot days. There'll usually be plenty of fluffy cumulus clouds lined up near the shore to prove what's going on. (Land gets hotter in the sunshine than water, hot air rises over the hot land, and cooler air moves in from over the water to replace it. In the evening, the process reverses as the land cools faster than the water, and cool air moves off the shore to replace air rising off the water.)

Wind is dirtied (turbulence) and weakened by shoreline obstructions—and also by islands, and fleets of boats or anything else that will interrupt its flow. Otherwise free-flowing wind gets interrupted by these obstructions, and eddies around them. When the wind is blowing offshore, it will be best alongside flat beaches and marshes; in the lee of cliffs or obstructions, there's a pocket of relatively dead and turbulent wind—stay away.

Many sailors pay less attention to the obstructions when the wind is blowing *onto* them—but they're nearly as important. A mass of relatively stagnant air gets piled up in front of the obstructions, and the flowing air hits this cushion, then rises off the water to get over the barrier. Result: poor wind in front of the obstruction—stay away.

Don't forget that a tightly packed fleet of sailboats is pretty much of an obstruction to the wind, so whether you're upwind or downwind, try to get away from the fleet.

Wind changes directions at shorelines, trying to cross the shore at right angles. This seems to be true whether the wind is onshore or offshore. The effect doesn't last very far, but if you sail in a small area where your courses run near shorelines, think about whether it will hurt or help to sneak over close enough to get a windshift. In light airs, this effect doesn't amount to much more than a hundred feet or so coming offshore, and half as far for onshore breezes. In heavier airs it's noticeable several times as far out. That's why you'll hear people talking about "picking up a lift near the shore" and sneaking ahead of a fleet. When you're near the shore, watch out for sudden gusts of wind resulting from the wind being funneled between tall buildings, or trees, or a canyon or rivermouth.

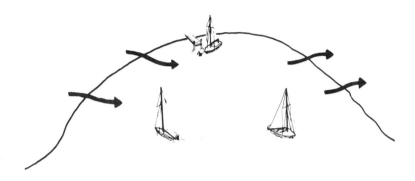

Look for windshifts near shorelines . . . generally, wind will tend to cross the shore at right angles.

Water currents are stronger in deep water, and weaker in shallow water. If you sail in tidal waters, where there's tide current one way or the other practically all of the time, you shouldn't ever race without a chart showing water depths all over your course. Then, when the tide's with you, route yourself over the deeper water; when it's not, scrape across the shallows.

If there aren't such charts for your area, or they don't give enough detail for your corner of the pond, the thing you ought to do is join a five-year-old child on a rainy day, and make sticks-and-stones dams in the gutter. Make a point of noticing the swirls and eddies that build up around points of "land" in the current flow. Float walnut-shell boats down the stream and make grown-up observations about where they go fast, where they go slow, and where they go backward. Play this muddy game enough, and you'll do all right about picking where to sail in a race.

6

Winning attitudes

If it ever enters your mind that the reason some skippers do a lot of winning while others don't is that they're naturally endowed with some special instinct, forget it! Every club has a skipper or two who're generally known as lucky rascals. They're not—they're better racers. There isn't anything the hotshot does that you can't do too. You can bet that the most important single thing he does that makes him hot is: he works at winning. Full time.

There are a few keys, and they'll work for anyone.

Use good equipment

Don't give away an edge by sailing a stupidly rigged boat with misfit sails and a dirty bottom. Any small boat's sails, if they're really out of shape, can be fixed up by a decent sailmaker for very modest charges—and in most small classes, a completely new set isn't all that much money for your recreation budget when you write them off over several summers' sailing. Ten or twenty dollars worth of line, blocks, and screws will rearrange the running rig on a dumbly rigged small boat, and a dollar's worth of wood will make you a new tiller extention if yours is too short. Ten dollars or so, and some elbow grease, will give you a slick racing bottom if yours is ratty. You haven't anything else to do all winter, anyway.

Sportsmanship and the rules

Second, don't try to compete outside the rules. The racing rules—and the resulting expectation that people will give a right-of-way when it's due—are the whole basis for practically all strategic maneuvering. I never heard of a sport that was any good without a rules structure, and that certainly includes sailing. When someone has right-of-way over you, make sure you let him have it. When you have right-of-way, enforce it; don't let a bluffer or who-cares type shove you out of it—if you do, you'll lose time and positions. That's what the rules are all about—figure your race to have the right-of-way at the starts, the marks, and all close-to-other-boats sailing, so that you can go ahead, not behind.

Don't make a thing out of the rules for their own sake. There will always be, in large fleets and small boats, tons of cases where little technical violations occur that have nothing to do with interfering with boats' progress or positions in the race. Overlook them, perhaps with a polite comment to the effect that you're glad you had the right-of-way, but this time it didn't matter. *But*, under a rule added in 1973, you should always protest when there's contact—otherwise you may be disqualified.

No one loves a sea-lawyer . . . but no one ever won races by saying "After you, Alphonse."

Try harder

Third, try harder . . . all of the time. When you're ahead, your job is to keep getting farther ahead; when you're behind, your job is to pass at least one boat.

There are, in every fleet, a bunch of skippers who enjoy a nice sociable ride around the course in good company with other skippers who are in the middle of the pack with them. They think that's lots of fun, and good company. They'd think it was more fun if they were in front.

There are three ways you should be trying. One is in making your boat do the best it can all the way through the course. This means constant attention to the trim of your sails—adjusting them for every change in wind strength or direction. It means constant attention to keeping your weight where it will do the most good. In short, one third of your attention, and about 90 percent of your crew's, should be on making the boat go. Another is in sailing your boat where it will do the most good—in better airs, better current, better position with regard to the next boat you'll meet on the course, better position at the start and at the marks. Third, try harder to get lucky.

The way you get lucky is by figuring out what could happen that would be lucky, and then making sure you're in a position where it can happen, or where if it happens it will happen for you more than for your opponent. When you're behind, think in terms of what kind of a wind shift could help you, and then go to where it's most likely to shift that way. If the only way you can catch the boat in front of you would be for him to swing wide at a mark (leaving you room to swing up inside of him), why not make sure you're in position, assuming he *will* goof it. If it will take an extra strong puff of wind to catch you up with a boat in front, make sure you're all set for that puff when it hits. As they say about football teams, "Make your own luck."

If your attitude's right about making some luck, you probably will—it's a self-fulfilling prophecy. The reason is, while you're in the process of thinking through how to get lucky, you'll likely stumble onto some bright idea that helps you without having to get lucky.

Sailsmanship

This is a sailor's final hope to confound his opponents. Someday I'm going to write a book about all the clean and dirty tricks I've run into on the water. Whether or not you want to use them, you sure have to be able to recognize them when they're aimed at you. Here are a few.

Hailing—which is polite talk for a lot of shouting—has a definite place in sailboat racing. For one case, when you're approaching another boat that has right-of-way over you, you really should hail him to let him know that you're planning to give way (and how you're going to do that). If you don't, there's a possibility that he'll shy away before you maneuver, and if he protests, you have a burden of proof which you'll usually lose; prevent his doing so by hailing. For another case, when approaching a mark at which you expect to rate buoy room, start hollering early to warn other boats that you're going to expect room—if you don't, and there are many boats there, the boat next to you may not be able to give room, even if he tries at the last minute. Better to hail early than miss the mark. For still another case, imagine you're right-of-way starboard tack boat about to meet a port tacker—hail "starboard tack." He may not see you, and winning a protest if he hits you really won't get you through the course as fast as sailing in clear water without hitting him—so hail, get him out of your way.

The dirty guys may hail you more than they need to do, perhaps hoping to bluff you out of a valid right-of-way, or simply hoping to get you rattled. When boats call for buoy room early, be forewarned but don't answer that you'll give it until they rate it (overlapped at two lengths' distance from the mark). When they overlap too late, tell 'em "too late." When a barger hails for room at the starting mark, you may be able to avoid a (time-costing) collision by hailing back "no room for bargers."

Hailing before any sharp or sudden maneuver or before reaching any crowded mess will let others know what you're up to and what rights you expect—it can save an awful lot of crashes, which in turn saves time.

Talking to other skippers during the race is used by some guys with the goal of distracting or confusing them. I used to know a regional champion whose favorite game, when following anyone downwind, would be to start up a conversation; he hoped that the leading skipper would turn to answer, getting his eyes off his sails and wind pennant—and if he was planning any attacking maneuver, he'd precede it with a "Look over there at (almost anything) . . ." and then zoom the minute he was sure the leader was looking the other way. He figured he got an extra 10 or 20 seconds of sneaking time that way. One way or another, he'd be sailing to win full time, while his opponent was busy gassing. You'd be surprised how often it worked.

Fending off boats when they're mashed together, as at messy starts, is an open invitation for dirty sailsmanship. When someone sticks his hand on your gunwale to fend you off, which way is he pushing? If it's a drifting match, a very slight shove in the wrong direction will kill you. Don't let anyone touch your boat, and don't touch any other boats. If you have to fend, do it with a life jacket or something, not your hand.

In a recent world's championship the pushing and shoving at the starts got so bad that one skipper blew his cork —the next guy who put a hand on his rail came away with broken fingers, after getting clobbered with a paddle. (The skipper who swung the paddle got suspended from racing for months—I think they punished the wrong man.)

Some more dirty sailsmanship: fiddling with the other guy's boat is not as rare as it should be. Especially in round-robin races where skippers swap off boats after each race, there's always the guy who tries to ruin the tuning of the boat he's in just before he leaves it. He'll goof up the out-haul tension, or halyards, or almost anything that he can easily change. I've seen raiders poking around the fleets at lunch time between races, and later found equipment loose or maladjusted. You hate to think it could happen in your club, but just in case, check your boat over before every start.

Some clean sailsmanship: decoying the lambs into bad starts is a favorite game for leaders in regattas and racing series. The leader (quite accurately) figures that all of the close contenders will be watching his pre-start maneuvering, trying to get his kind of start. So what he does is to wander around the line trying to look as if he's practicing whatever he isn't going to do—if he plans to start at the starboard end, he makes practice drives at the port end; if he plans to do a dip-start, he makes dry runs at the windward corner. Pretty much the same game: the hotshot who wants to sneak along the shoreline takes off in the opposite direction for long enough to lure the followers onto the bad area—then when he swings over to the shore, he hopes the followers are committed and in a crowd, leaving him to go alone.

Some more clean sailsmanship: toward the latter part of any regatta or race series, there's usually only one boat that you really have to beat. Learn to keep track of standings and scores, and to know who you have to beat—and who has to beat you. When such a situation develops, the winning skipper learns to keep his eye off the fleet and on the opponent who counts. The start becomes a match race between those two boats, and so does the rest of the course. Don't be surprised someday when you find one boat that seems dedicated to ruining your start, circling to put himself between you and wherever you want to be, and generally being a nuisance—he may know just what he's doing, and he just *may* be hoping you'll foul him.

Now that you know his game, you can almost always shake him off by mixing in with the crowded part of the fleet—do it early enough to leave time to get back by yourself before starting. When you're the aggressor, trying to beat just one boat, the best general advice is to sail your own race for a good start, and thereafter cover him if you're ahead (disregarding the rest of the fleet—that usually takes care of itself) and doing your darndest to avoid cover if he's ahead. There are books on fancy techniques for match-race starting, but they're for the very advanced skipper and usually don't work worth a hoot in the middle of a fleet of small boats. Forget it, and start well.

One other point on sailsmanship: it always seems to end at the dock. I can't ever remember running into a top skipper who wasn't completely free and open, after the race, about sharing with anyone who asked all the details about how he rigged and tuned, how he started, where he sailed, and why. Not only are racers cordial about sharing their ideas, they seem in general to be downright anxious to improve the competition for the next race by doing all they can to help others learn. Feel free to ask the leaders in your fleet for advice on everything from where to tuck your toes when hiking to where the wind blows best around Pintail Island. The one thing that doesn't seem to end at the dock is the resentment toward skippers who violated racing rules—and that's no problem if you'll learn the rules. When you're not sure of the rules, stay clear.

A succinct summary of several secrets for sailing success

Start on time at the favored end or near it. Compromise a little bit, giving up a few lengths from the favored corner if necessary to get clear air.

Maxi-tack, playing the temporary windshifts so as to sail always on the lifted tack, never the headed tack.

Sail the boat flat; better to spill wind than to let it heel.

Shun "salt pork" (that's a boat that is a pig); keep the bottom clean, rigging fit, and don't try to compete outside of sandboxes without good sails. Better to trade down into a cheaper boat than to strive in one you can't keep up really right.

Winning is: doing everything you know, all of the time. Be speedy and greedy.

Appendix A

How to rig the boat for
the wind of the day

First we'll discuss setting up the sails, because they're the most important part, being your only source of power.

Remember: your general principle in *bending* sails (that is, mounting them, as distinguished from setting their position to the wind for the moment) is simply this: *the harder the wind blows, the tighter she goes.* That really applies to just about all the adjustments you have. Let's look at what's available to adjust:

Halyard
Gooseneck downhaul and/or Cunningham
Clew outhaul
Boom vang
Backstay
Jib luff wire

Example of a well-designed "office" — the crew station on Megan, *Bob Shaughnessy's E-22. Jibsheets are led to the midships winch and then to the windward clamcleat. Reading from left to right, the jam-cleated lines are: Barber-hauler (for starboard jibsheet), foreguy, jibstay tension, spinnaker halyard, boom vang, Cunningham tension, topping lift, jib (cloth) downhaul, and Barber-hauler (for the port jibsheet).*

Pressure batten, several inches longer than the sail's pocket, can be tied in loosely (for flatter sail) or it may be "sprung" in — tied under tension — to increase the curvature of the upper sail. It should be tied loosely in a blow, under pressure in light airs.

Halyard. The mainsail should be hoisted as high as it can go to the top of the mast. On many classes of boats, there's a legal limit, which is marked with a black band near the top of the mast. Hoist to there. If there isn't such a limit, hoist to the top (except that, on some rigs, hoisting the very last inch or so will put a strain on the headboard of the sail, causing wrinkles). When hoisting, make sure there's nothing fastened at the bottom to hold it down (such as boom vang, boom downhaul, or cleated mainsheet), then hoist, check for wrinkles, and if there are a lot of wrinkles' near the head, try letting the halyard back down an inch or two; if the wrinkles don't go away, hoist back up anyway.

After sailing a while make a mental note to check your halyard, if it isn't wire, because it will stretch and may need to be retightened.

Gooseneck downhaul and Cunningham. Most boats have adjustable gooseneck rigs (the fitting where the mast and boom meet). Most of the newer ones also have a "Cunningham" rig, which is a grommeted hole in the sail about a foot above the gooseneck, by which the luff of the sail (forward edge) may be stretched tighter (downward).

If you do have a Cunningham, set the downhaul to place the sail's foot at the black band and forget it—use the Cunningham for tension. (If there's no black band, set the downhaul so the sail's luff is just snug.)

If you don't have a Cunningham, use the downhaul to set tension. Either way, the principle is the same . . . the heavier the wind, the more tension. In light airs, just snug (no Cunningham tension used). In moderately good wind, pull her down a bit but not enough to cause major wrinkling of the sail. When it's blowing hard, haul it down until it's as tight as seems possible without damaging the sail; that'll be about 20 to 30 pounds' pull on a 15-footer, and five times that on a 30-footer.

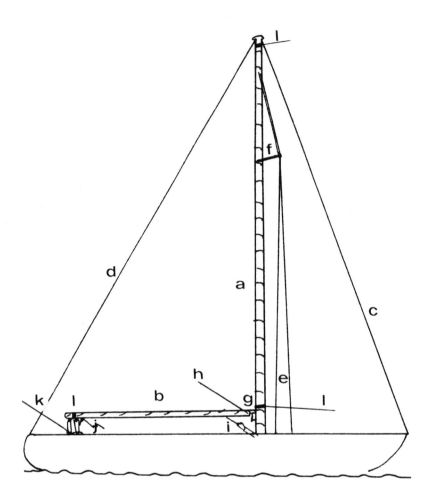

A   Mast . . . main vertical spar
B   Boom . . . horizontal spar
C   Headstay . . . forward support
    for mast; also "jibstay"
D   Backstay . . . aft support
    for mast
E   Shrouds . . . athwartship support
    for mast
F   Spreaders . . . position shrouds
    for better angle
G   Gooseneck . . . hardward joining
    mast and boom

H   Downhaul . . . rigging to tension
    gooseneck downward
I   Boom vang . . . rigging to hold
    boom down
J   Mainsheet . . . rigging to
    position boom, thus setting
    mainsail to best angle
K   Traveller . . . rigging to
    adjust angle of mainsheet pull
L   Black bands . . . marks at masthead,
    gooseneck, and boom end showing
    legal (measured) limits for sail

Outhaul. The clew outhaul, which pulls the sail out to the end of the boom, follows the same general principle—the harder the wind blows, the tighter she goes. There's a fair bit of judgment involved in finding the right outhaul tension, which you'll develop with experience. For starters, you might try about one half to one pound pull in very light winds (under 5 mph), about two to three pounds pull in middle winds (up to around 15 mph), and say ten pounds pull in higher winds.

Remember that it's illegal to pull the sail out past the black band, if your class has such limits.

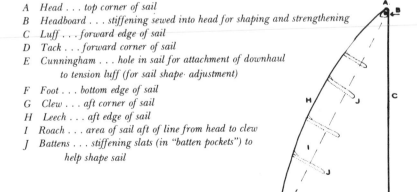

A Head . . . top corner of sail
B Headboard . . . stiffening sewed into head for shaping and strengthening
C Luff . . . forward edge of sail
D Tack . . . forward corner of sail
E Cunningham . . . hole in sail for attachment of downhaul
    to tension luff (for sail shape· adjustment)

F Foot . . . bottom edge of sail
G Clew . . . aft corner of sail
H Leech . . . aft edge of sail
I Roach . . . area of sail aft of line from head to clew
J Battens . . . stiffening slats (in "batten pockets") to
    help shape sail

There's a current trend toward an *inhaul* rig that works just like the Cunningham, only tightens the foot of the sail by hauling a grommet in toward the gooseneck. If you have such a rig, use that for tension instead of the outhaul—just set the outhaul to place the sail at the black band and leave it there.

Boom vang. Most racing classes come equipped with some sort of vang. While its main function is to keep the boom down when you're sailing with the wind, the vang also has some effect on the shape of the sail when you're close-hauled. The general rule is that of the other adjustments —loose in light air, tight in heavy winds. For a simple rule of thumb, until you've had a chance to feel for yourself what makes your boat go, try setting the vang so that it's about three times as tight as whatever tension you've decided on for the outhaul. Watch out when setting it— most boats provide some sort of "power" (block-and-tackle leverage) to the vang, and if you overdo things you can put a tremendous strain on the equipment. If your boat doesn't have a vang, it's wise to check with skippers experienced in the class before setting one up, to be sure you won't pull equipment apart.

Boom vang keeps downward pressure on boom when sailing off the wind — thus preventing the upper part of the sail from sagging forward. Little or no tension needed close-hauled (as the mainsheet exerts enough downward pull in this position); reaching and downwind, apply enough tension to align the aft end of the top-most batten parallel with the boom. If the batten "hooks" to windward, there's too much downward tension; if it sags to leeward, there's too little.

When things are blowing up, be very sure to have the vang set up taut while the mainsheet is tightly close-hauled. You'll find that the sheet puts a bend in the boom, letting some slack onto a vang that was set up at the dock when there was no pressure. You want the vang quite tightly set *before* you fall off onto the downwind legs of the course. There's where the boom would otherwise rise up somewhat (being no longer subject to downward pressure from the mainsheet), allowing the sail to bag at the roach—with the result that the upper third or so of the sail would sag forward and lose effectiveness. The vang pressure keeps the sail in shape when sailing downwind.

Jib halyard. On many of the smaller boats, the jib halyard will be the only adjustment available to you on the jib. Follow the same rule—the heavier it blows, the tighter she goes. *But only up to a point.* You're going to end up in a conflict of interests, and this is why: tightening the luff of the jib will improve its heavy-weather shape, *but* it will also tend to pull the mast forward. On the other hand, having the mast bend aft somewhat will improve the shape of the mainsail in heavy winds, and that's more important in most boats. Conclusion—let the jib have a full-shape, easy (low-tension) hoist in light airs, and give it a-bit-more-than-snug in heavier winds, but don't really stretch it out tight. Mast bending will do that for you.

Jib halyard tension can be adjusted to rake the mast. (In boats equipped with adjustable backstays, the backstays perform the function better.) In this 470 rig, the halyard ends in a wire loop (A); lever arm (B) may be easily set with its fulcrum in a range of positions (C). Tension changes cause the mast to rake fore-and-aft, helping flatten or deepen the draft (curvature) in the mainsail. Rake forward (for full mainsail) in light air, rake aft (for flatter mainsail) in a blow.

If you have backstay adjustments available, then bend the mast with them and go ahead and tension the jib halyard just as you would the main· halyard or gooseneck downhaul.

Backstay. If you have an adjustable backstay, use it to bend the mast backward at the top in heavier winds when beating to windward. In light airs and when going downwind, let it off enough to straighten the mast. The curved shape that the backstays produce in the upper portion of the mast helps the mainsail to develop a more effective shape in higher winds.

Jibsheets. Many classes permit the use of adjustable fairleads by which you can alter the angle from the clew of the jib to the deck—which in turn can help form the best shape in the jib. Nowadays, the most popular rigs involve a *fairlead track,* by which you can slide the fairlead fore-and-aft, plus a *Barber-hauler* by which you can adjust the sheeting angle inboard-outboard (athwartship). Use of these adjustments is discussed on page 21, under Sailsetting.

a   *Jib sheets . . . rigging to position jib*
b   *Jib sheet fairlead . . . pulley or deadeye to control sheeting angle*
c   *Track and slides . . . rigging to allow for fairlead adjustment, usually fore-and-aft*
d   *Barber-hauler . . . rigging to adjust jib sheeting angle athwartships (shown slack)*

Reefing. Many boats can be reefed—that is, you can shorten the mainsail by rolling it up on the boom, or by tying up the lower portion into a bundle just over the boom. The purpose, of course, is to make the boat more manageable in heavy winds which would otherwise force you to heel excessively and to deliberately luff the sails, spilling wind.

Sails aren't too expensive on small boats; you're much, much better off to own a (smaller) second sail for heavy weather. It will perform a great deal better for you than will a reefed sail. But before you buy a second sail, check your class rules, as some classes forbid it (in the interests of keeping the cost of racing down).

If you're going to have to reef the mainsail, for goodness' sake do so before the race gets started. It's a great deal easier to shake out a reef you don't need than to put in a reef you do need. Obviously, you want all the sail working you can stand when you're racing, so only reef when you really can't keep the boat sailing without it. If you can sail the boat *most* of the time without spilling wind out of the sails to avoid capsizing or excessive heeling, don't reef—just spill some wind when you must; if you have to spill wind most of the time, you'll race better with the sail reefed.

Standing rigging. Shrouds and stays (the wires that hold the mast in position) need to be set up right in the first place, and then "tuned" from time to time during the season. Although many beginners tend to take them for granted, only a moment's thought will convince you that they are important. After all, they control the shape of the mast, which in turn shapes the mainsail.

The principle of setting the standing rigging is to assure that the mast stays straight in the thwartships directions, neither sagging off to leeward nor bending in the center with the tip arcing up to windward. Some boats also sail best with the mast straight in the fore-and-aft axis, but more of the modern sails are so cut that having the upper portion of the mast bend aft somewhat as the wind becomes stronger helps to get the best mainsail shape. (This bending is generally done automatically by the downward pull of the mainsheet on the boom, perhaps assisted by adding some tension to the backstay if you have one.)

"Tuning" a mast, by adjusting the standing rigging, is largely a trial-and-error business. The right way to get started is to get the advice of the fleet champion in your area. You know you need adjustments if:

- the mast sags off to leeward in a blow; tighten the windward shrouds.
- the mast arcs, with the tip bending toward the windward side; loosen the windward shrouds.
- the mast bends with the tip going forward, the center arcing aft; loosen the headstay.

Any shroud that doesn't have a little play in it when the boat is at the dock is too tight; a shroud with more than three or four inches' play when wiggled back and forth is probably too loose.

If the mast will not bend aft at the tip in a blow (and others in the class do) try raking it just a bit. Do this by moving the foot of the mast forward (half an inch or an inch at a try) or by giving a bit more slack to the headstay. Also consider that you may be hoisting the jib too tightly.

If you have a complex mast, with two or more shrouds on each side and/or with adjustable spreaders, do get the advice of experienced racers in the class; your boat is bound to have unique tuning tricks. Spend part of lunch time at your next regatta looking over how others set their masts.

Remember that if you have backstays, they adjust with the wind, and the old rule holds: the harder it blows, the tighter she goes.

Bottom finish. This is one more item in keeping a boat fit to race: the *bottom must be clean.* In small boats, there's nothing to it—just take the boat over to the beach or haul it up on the dock, and turn to with a sponge and soap or *very fine* steel wool. If you keep up with it, scrubbing every week or so, it shouldn't take more than five minutes to do the boat.

People are still arguing about what's the best bottom finish for racing boats. The very fact that there's something to argue about proves that no one has yet found the right answer—*or* it proves that it really doesn't make very much difference. All the evidence I have so far has convinced me that the kind of bottom finish doesn't matter, as long as it's clean and feels smooth to your fingertips. If it makes you feel better, go ahead and wax, or polish, or whatever—feeling better makes a faster skipper—but in any event, keep it clean. Fill in deep scratches with plastic putty and sand it smooth. Smooth out little scratches with fine (number 600) wet-or-dry sandpaper used wet. And keep it clean.

The same obviously applies to centerboards, keels, rudders, or anything else that's under water.

Centerboard and rudder shaping is illegal in an increasing number of classes (and so it should be, just as is altering hull shape!) in the interest of keeping boats "one design." If that's true of your class, then go easy on the sandpaper.

If your class permits shaping—and the boat builder didn't do it for you—it's very worthwhile to get both blades into a smooth, elongated teardrop shape. Don't fall into the common temptation of going for a knife-sharp front edge to the blades—it's in fact much less efficient than a blunt curve. The place for the sharp edge is at the trailing edge of the blades, where it will help the flowing water to come together smoothly.

Blade shaping (centerboards, rudders)

Wrong.

Chisel-shaped edges do not flow smoothly through the water.

Right.

Elongated tear-drop with blunt forward edge, sharp trailing edge is efficient both when going straight and when turning.

Appendix B

Rigging a Sunfish to Race

The lateen rig of the Sunfish, with no modifications allowed under class rules, still needs some rigging attention. Being the largest class around, it's an excellent boat for learning to race. But if you don't set it up right, you're unlikely to do well. Here are the essentials.

A *Mainsheet snapped to port of eye in bridle*

B *Tiller extension handle "not to exceed 2 inches" (made from spare sail set)*

A *Foremost sail set removed from foot of sail*

B *Gooseneck relocated slightly aft of factory mark (black tape)*

C *Deck-mounted compass*

E *Block for mainsheet (replaces "cup hook" open fairlead)*

F *Jam cleats for mainsheet*

G *Window in sail*

Lower the rig by tying the halyard farther up the yard (the hoisted spar) than the conventional midpoint. About nine-and-one-half rings up from the bottom is a good place for most people—perhaps half-a-ring lower for light airs, just beneath the tenth ring for very windy days.

Level the boom just a bit by relocating the gooseneck an inch or two farther back than the factory location. The average position for leading boats at the 1972 North American Championships was about 23 inches from the bolt-eye that joins the spars up forward.

Set the luff tension at not-quite-snug by pulling the sail out to the end of the yard (vertical spar), then letting it have about an inch of slack before tying it. Some of the hotshots vary this tension with wind and sea conditions, but the absence of agreement as to how to set it strongly suggests that it doesn't much matter.

Set the foot tension at pretty-darn-loose—about three inches less than snug. On really windy days, pull it out to snug but not taut.

Remove the foremost "sail set" (nylon clip) on the boom; this allows the sail to take a somewhat better shape up forward where there should be some curvature.

Mount a block or fairlead to pass the mainsheet at or near the forward edge of the cockpit (where the factory-mounted "cup hook" open fairlead is found) and use it. Most racers mount the sort that includes a jam-cleat feature, or as an alternative mount jam cleats on either side of a conventional block. Unless the sheet is run down to this position, the pull on the sheet will cause some excess lateral bending of the boom; pulling downward to this central location produces boom-bending that improves the shape of the sail, especially when it blows up harder.

Move the sheet-to-bridle clip over to the port side of the bridle, instead of clipping to the loop of the bridle, especially whenever the wind is blowing hard. This helps avoid excessive heeling on starboard tack, when the clip slides off to the corner; on port tack the clip slides over to set at the loop, but the mast "spoils" the sail some and eases forces on that tack.

Make sure the halyard is taut where the yard meets the masthead; the original equipment cotton line stretches for a while, and when it gets loose aloft, the rig sags away from the mast on starboard tack, ruining your ability to point. Recheck this tension before every race start, especially when the wind's up—or replace the line with something of the same size that won't stretch.

Rig a centerboard holder that will allow you to set the daggerboard at any depth you like, and leave it there. The standard rig is the simplest: mount a screw-eye at the top of the board, and stretch a shock cord from it to the mast or halyard; the tension makes the board stay put very nicely.

For everything in the world about how to race a Sunfish, get a copy of *Sail It Flat* by Larry Lewis with Chuck Millican (Quadrangle Press).

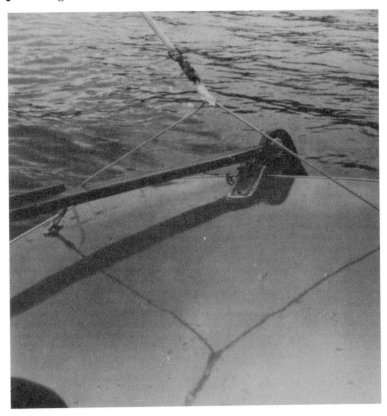

The function of a tiller stop can be served by a traveller of the bridle type if, kept taut with mainsheet tension while tacking — note how the tiller of this Sunfish is up against the traveller.

Appendix C

Ulmer/Stanton on Sail & Air

A treatment of the aerodynamics of sailing by Charles Ulmer & John Stanton

Introduction

The physics of sails are not particularly complex; yet, even today, broad differences of opinion about the subject continue to exist. As a result, the design of sails is more art than science, a craft which places great emphasis upon intuition and experience.

The present state of sail development has evolved through centuries of trial and error. Now it is becoming evident that continued improvement in sail performance will become increasingly more dependent upon analytical design and refinement of materials and manufacturing techniques.

Plan-form

The genesis of nearly all modern sail plans is the Marconi rig. The triangular shaped fore-and-aft rig offers, for the present, the best compromise between the hull, sail, and mast requirements.

Marconi rigs have proved to be effective on all points of sailing. Under favorable circumstances they point within three and one-half points (40 degrees) of the true wind, while spinnakers and related running sails approach the idealized sail configuration for downwind sailing.

Airfoil Section Characteristics

The term "airfoil" applies equally to a strapped-down genoa or a spinnaker. The flow characteristics are very different; nevertheless, each is an airfoil and should be treated as such, according to its own unique circumstances.

Modern sails have two basic section profiles. When close-hauled: jib, genoa, main, and mizzen profiles are parabolic in shape; the maximum camber, or draft, should be 8 to 12 percent. The location of maximum camber ranges from 20 to 50 percent of chord length according to type.

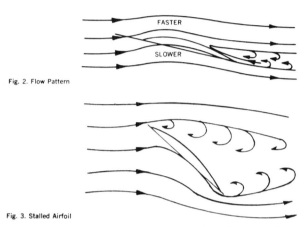

Fig. 2. Flow Pattern

Fig. 3. Stalled Airfoil

As the craft falls off the wind on to a reach, the camber is increased 3 to 5 percent by adjusting sheets, down-hauls, and, on occasion, zippers or slab reefs.

In both of the cases enumerated so far, the airfoil lies in planes which are inclined to the apparent wind. This condition is referred to as the "angle of attack" in aerodynamics. The streamlines which pass over the convex or leeward surface are accelerated to a higher velocity. The streamlines passing over the concave or windward surface may actually experience a slight decrease in velocity. The resultant pressure differential is classic and is referred to as the Bernoulli principle.

Fig. 4. Aerodynamic Force Vectors

It is normal aerodynamic practice to reduce the dynamic force into components which are perpendicular and parallel, respectively, to the apparent wind. The point at which the components and resultant forces react is the center of pressure. These components are labeled "lift" and "drag." (See Figure 4.)

When broad-reaching and running, each sail is fully stalled, which is the aerodynamicist's way of saying that severe flow separation is present on the leeward side by the sail. The resultant aerodynamic force is the result of drag. The maximum drag force occurs with an ellipsoidal cross-section and a depth-to-width ratio of 35 percent. Spinnakers cut to this shape maximize the product of the drag coefficient times the projected area and, therefore, the spinnaker pulling power.

The mainsail presents a problem of a different sort. In order to be effective on all points of sailing, the sail designer and the yachtsman must resort to a variety of camber control devices and adjustment techniques. These include zippers, reefs, leech lines, down-hauls, Cunningham holes, and clew out-haul and halyard tension adjustment.

The mainsail, versatile as it is, cannot provide maximum efficiency on all points of sailing. Windward performance is most sensitive to sail shape and set; consequently, the mainsail is designed to optimize its close-hauled characteristics. Camber control devices allow the yachtsman to increase fullness when running or reaching. The resultant cross-section and depth, when running, are usually parabolic with a camber ratio on the order of 15 to 20 percent of chord; the maximum camber should occur at about the 50 percent chord point.

Three-Dimensional Flow

The airflow phenomena which we have considered so far have been two-dimensional only. A practical airfoil is three-dimensional, which radically alters the rather simple aerodynamics associated with the two-dimensional state.

In yachting circles it has been the custom to let aspect ratio be defined as the ratio of the sail height to the sail foot. Unfortunately, this fails to take into account the shape of the sail.

Even the aerodynamicist's definition loses some of its

meaning when applied to sails. Classic three-dimensional flow theory has been developed for symmetrical airfoils without tip constraints. The Marconi rig exemplifies the exception to the ideal airfoil. It is nonsymmetrical; flow at the foot is restricted; the sail twists from foot to head; the air velocity is not uniform, being somewhat higher at the head than the foot. Nevertheless, three-dimensional theory, when properly adjusted to account for sail asymmetry, provides an accurate analysis of the aerodynamics involved.

Fig. 6 Trailing Vortices

Fig. 7. Definition of Downwash

A finite airfoil in a free stream experiences a lateral flow vector from the high pressure region, around the tips, to the low pressure area. This circulatory flow produces vortices which trail the tips and influence the streamlines passing over the airfoil. (See Figure 6.)

The circulatory air motion also introduces a negative flow, commonly referred to as "downwash," along the trailing edge. Downwash has a profound effect upon overlapping and tandem sails as we shall see later. (See Figure 7.)

The spanwise aerodynamic loading of a sail is relatively complex. The load distribution is strongly influenced by the sail profile; nevertheless, factors such as tip effect, twist, varying sections velocity gradient and mast interference alter the pattern, especially near the boom and head.

The "ideal" sail has a load distribution similar in shape to the sail outline or plan-form. This represents the maximum potential aerodynamic force which is theoretically available from any given sail. The various influences itemized in the previous paragraph all tend to decrease sail performance to such a degree that the actual aerodynamic

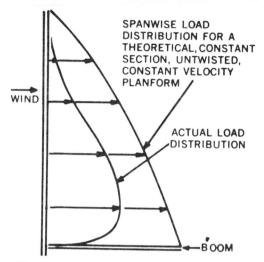

Fig 8. Load Distribution for an Ideal Sail & a Real Sail. (Curves altered slightly for clarity).

loading of a Marconi-rigged sail is about one half of the "ideal" value. (See Figure 8.)

In theory the P/B ratio should be extremely high. As a practical matter, however, mast staying, interference and rating penalties limit the ratio to values of 2 or 3 to 1. We shall examine the latter influence in a subsequent paragraph.

Sail Characteristics "On The Wind"

Classical low speed aerodynamics define an ideal airfoil as being symmetrical, elliptical in plan-form, and free of aerodynamic and geometric twist. It is quite obvious that the Marconi airfoil falls far short of the classic airfoil. Let us examine some of the differences between an ideal airfoil and a Marconi rigged sail.

The proximity of the boom to the hull and sea influences the induced flow around the foot of the sail. In effect, the hull and sea act as a barrier which greatly impede the flow from the weather to the lee side of the sail. The result is a significant increase in lift and a decrease in drag over the lower region of the sail.

In the past, some designers adopted the practice of rais-
ing the boom height to a level well above current values
in an effort to reach higher velocity undisturbed air and
to reduce sail area, thereby lowering the rating. These
efforts can be self-defeating since the higher center of
effort impairs sail carrying ability, and the increased flow
around the boom offsets the increased wind velocity.

Fig. 9. The Effect of Twist on Angle of Attack

A well-designed and set Marconi sail normally has 15 to
20 degrees of geometric twist between the boom and headboard when close-hauled. This condition is known in
aerodynamics as "washout." It immediately becomes obvious
that the foot of the sail must be sheeted-in hard in order
for the head to develop any driving force. Twist occurs as
the result of stretch in the sailcloth thread lines which lie
parallel to the leech. Some twist is desirable since the apparent wind at the head lies more "abeam" than at the foot.

Sail Characteristics "Off The Wind"

When broad-reaching and running, the Marconi mainsail
is set to maximize drag. (See Figure 3.) The clew outhaul
and halyard are slackened, the leech line tightened; and the
zipper or reef, if available, is loosened. These actions all
tend to increase the fullness of the sail. Mainsails, as cur-
rently fabricated, seldom, if ever, achieve the optimum
downwind configuration.

The ideal downwind sail has a projected area aspect ratio
of 1.275. A circular flat plate, a hemisphere, or an oblate
hemispheroid (i.e., a parachute) are three prime examples

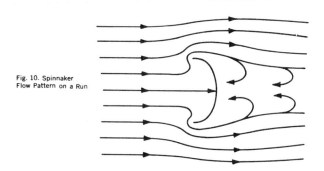

Fig. 10. Spinnaker
Flow Pattern on a Run

of "airfoils" which possess this characteristic.

The spinnaker is a fair imitation of a parachute. As such, it approaches but never attains parachute levels of performance. Nevertheless, the spinnaker is a powerful sail and is a "must" in the sail inventory of the racing yachtsman.

The ideal running rig is a huge broad-shouldered spinnaker hoisted to the masthead, the tack sheeted through a spinnaker pole to the afterdeck and the clew sheeted through the end of the boom to the afterdeck. No additional sails would be flown (in the case of a sloop) which would permit the spinnaker to develop its full drive unimpeded.

The single huge spinnaker rig is not permissible under most contemporary rating rules. One might also ask the very practical question, "Could a sail of such huge proportions be adequately handled?"

Sail Interaction

The yachtsman should consider sail interaction whenever two or more sails are set. This rule applies without exception.

The most common and most important example of sail interaction in modern yachting is the combination of genoa jib and mainsail. The genoa, because of its size and unimpeded as it is by mast turbulence, is an extremely powerful and effective sail. Properly sheeted, the foot should be at the stall point which is the point of maximum lift or lateral force. At the head, the angle of attack will be about one half that of the foot. As a rule of thumb, the yachtsman can expect the genoa to provide at least twice as much driving power per square foot of area when compared to the mainsail. Genoas on many craft, especially those with masthead fore triangles, are larger than the mainsails and therefore develop two to three times the mainsail driving force.

The influence of the mainsail on a working jib is small. An overlapping jib, such as a genoa, gains appreciably due to increased wind velocity. The close proximity of the mainsail to the genoa lengthens the effective genoa chord so that the actual chord lies within the higher velocity flow region characteristic of the forward section of a normal airfoil. An effective velocity increase over the genoa of 10 to 15 percent is common.

Fig. 12. Sail Interaction

The genoa exerts a profound influence upon the mainsail. It is to be hoped that the reader will accept this statement as fact while we proceed to document it:

1. Any fore-and-aft headsail, when properly set, acts as a guide vane to coerce the apparent wind to flow over the leeward surface of the mainsail without separating (except for mast turbulence).

2. The downwash streaming from the leech of the jib induces further turning of the apparent wind which delays flow separation. The genoa jib is particularly effective in this manner because its downwash flows into the aft portions of the mainsail foot section, the area most prone to flow separation. (See Figures 8 and 12).

3. There is a small increase in velocity over the lee of the mainsail. For example, at 15 knots, the increase in flow velocity due to the so-called nozzle effect amounts to 3 to 4 percent, which increases the aerodynamic load proportionately.

Headsail and mainsail sheeting assume increasing importance with each incremental extension of overlap. It is
essential that the airstream leaving the genoa leech flow
parallel to slightly convergent to the adjacent mainsail section. A strongly convergent flow will "backwind" the mainsail and reduce its effectiveness. A divergent flow results
in a loss of genoa driving force.

The genoa trim angle is largely determined by the
amount of overlap and the location of the trimming point.
A beamy boat is more favorable for optimum genoa trim
since it provides for a greater variety of athwartship adjustment of the genoa sheet lead block.

A long overlapping genoa must be sheeted with the clew
positioned well aft, which restricts the variation of genoa
trim angle. Sail interaction becomes more retrogressive as
the genoa trim angle approaches the mainsail trim angle.
As a general rule, the genoa trim angle should be at least
5 degrees greater than the mainsail trim as measured at the
boom.

A genoa trim angle of 12 degrees, as measured between
the chord line and the centerline of the boat, is about the
ideal setting for most craft. With the boom trimmed to 5
degrees, the craft should foot handsomely on a course of
40 to 45 degrees off the true wind.

Finally, the yachtsman should consider the rating
penalties associated with genoa L.P.'s in excess of 150 percent. In many boats the maximum thrust is achieved with
a 160 or 170 percent L.P. genoa. Some even go as high
as 190 percent. If the thrust curve CTA has a flat characteristic, the skipper should select the L.P. which reduces his
rating and maximizes his speed. (See Figure 13.)

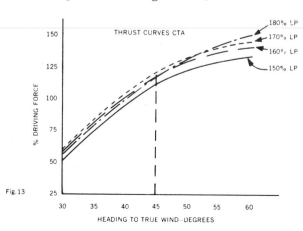

Fig. 13

Sail interaction also exists on other points of sailing. The most notable example, when reaching or running, is the spinnaker and mainsail.

In normal usage the spinnaker is hoisted and sheeted so that 35 to 40 percent of its projected area is in the lee of the mainsail. As a result the spinnaker is unable to develop its full driving potential. On the other hand, the aspect ratio of the spinnaker-mainsail combination more nearly approaches the optimum rectangular aspect ratio of 1.0; this partially offsets the effect of the mainsail blanketing on the leech of the spinnaker.

The tack of the spinnaker should be set as far as possible from the mast to maximize projected area. The clew should be sheeted to permit unimpeded flow around the leech of the spinnaker and to maximize the sail area exposed to the apparent wind. This will provide the maximum driving force for the mainsail-spinnaker combination. The reader should study the flow pattern for a typical mainsail-spinnaker combination as shown in Figure 14.

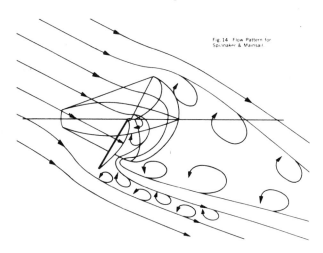

Fig. 14 Flow Pattern for Spinnaker & Mainsail.

Induced Trailing Flow

Another form of induced flow is present in multiple mast craft such as yawls, ketches, and schooners. It is the result of "Downwash" which was briefly described in an earlier paragraph and Figure 7. Downwash is a phenomenon in which the wind direction and velocity in the vicinity of an airfoil are altered by the flow streaming from the trailing edge of the foil. Thus, the mizzen on a yawl, when trimmed at the same angle as the main, develops a smaller lateral force coefficient.

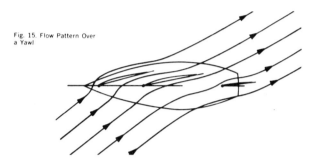

Fig. 15. Flow Pattern Over a Yawl

Optimum shape and trim of a mizzen when "on the wind" is attained with a slightly flatter cut sail than the main, the maximum camber located between 45 and 50 percent chord, and 1 to 2 degrees closer trimmed than the main.

Heeling Effect Upon Sail Characteristics

Wind has a profound effect upon sail performance. As the craft heels, the apparent angle of attack is reduced. For example, a geometric angle of attack of 20 degrees in the upright position becomes 18.9 degrees when the vessel heels to 20 degrees.

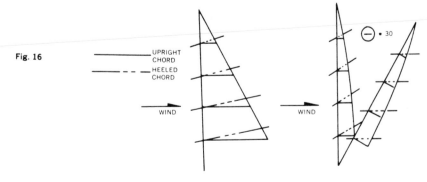

Fig. 16

As a yacht heels under the pressure of the aerodynamic load on the sails, the section profiles which the apparent wind traverses also change. The effective profiles are inclined slightly around an apex located at the luff. Since the sail sags to leeward, the shift of the section trailing edge must move outboard. The section angle of attack is further reduced (very slightly); and, in some cases, the effective camber is altered.

Figure 16 graphically describes the effect of heeling on sail section profile.

The Effects of Masts on Sail Performance

The mast, boom, and standing and running rigging all influence yacht performance. The mast has by far the greatest impact upon sail performance. We shall therefore limit the current discussion to the mast and its influence on yacht performance.

Figure 17 gives a graphic illustration of the air flow around a circular mast. Note that flow separation occurs on the lee side of the mast.

Fig. 17. Flow Past a Circular Mast

The extent to which sail performance is affected by the mast is a function of the shape of the mast and the mast diameter/chord ratio. Typical masts are oval or rectangular with large corner radii. Some are streamlined, and a few are round.

Flow over the mast separates from the surface shortly after traversing the apparent maximum width. The separation flow sets in motion a series of trailing vortices which increase pressure, reduce suction on the lee side of the sail, and reduce dynamic pressure on the weather side. Maximum intensity occurs about one mast diameter downstream from the luff.

Fig. 18. Comparison of Wakes for Equivalent Masts

At apparent wind angles in excess of 30 degrees, the widths of the wakes swept out by oval, rectangular, or streamlined masts are greater than that of an equivalent circular mast. From a purely aerodynamic point of view the round mast generally offers advantages while close-hauled or reaching over other nonrotatable masts. (See Figure 18.)

Sail Performance

Variations in the angle between the course sailed and the true wind produce significant changes in the developed driving force and heeling force for any given boat. Changes in these forces should be fully understood and appreciated by all sailing buffs.

Performance "on the wind" is the most critical measure of a sail's performance. At this condition it is particularly sensitive to shape, angle of attack, apparent wind, heel, interaction, etc. As the boat falls off the wind, the apparent wind velocity is reduced, which diminishes the total areodynamic load. Simultaneously, the heeling and driving force vectors are altered to provide a greater driving force. Initially the decreased aerodynamic loading is more than compensated for by the increased driving force ratio.

As the boat falls farther off the wind onto broad reaching and running, the apparent wind, and therefore the total force and driving force, decrease until a minimum level is reached.

A sail polar diagram is a very effective means of illustrating the variation in driving force over the entire range of headings. If a figure of merit of 100 percent is assigned as the measure of a well-designed suit of sails on a true course of 40 degrees, the relative driving force can be displayed on a polar diagram at all other conditions.

Figure 19 illustrates the relative driving force for a displacement sailing yacht in a moderate breeze.

Fig. 19. Typical Driving Force Polar

Fig. 20

Heavy-Weather Genoas

Probably the least understood, yet in their own right the most important sails on an ocean-racing yacht are heavy-weather genoas, specifically its #2 and #3. Since these sails are not their last resort in "survival" conditions, many skippers don't realize the importance of their proper design, cut, and construction.

The common conception of a proper #2 and #3 is a sail of slightly heavier cloth than the #1, with substantial overlap and a shortened luff (Figure 20). This, so the theory goes, lowers the center of effort to reduce heel and maintains overlap (and thus slot effect) to give the boat maximum drive.

Nothing could be further from the truth! To understand this fully, let's consider the above paragraph item by item.

First of all, today's boats, particularly those with light displacement, have high ballast displacement ratios and, through wider beams and hull configurations, they develop a tremendous amount of stability from their hulls. Both these factors lead to greater loading on sails. Thus substantially heavier cloth weights are indicated in order to maintain proper shape. My own experience in this year's SORC bears this out.

Fig. 21

Wind

Msl-Boom approx. midships
Msl-Boom with traveler out

Fig. 22

Genoa
in both positions
as in figure 2
Note:
1. Opened slot
2 No backwind

Msl in both position
as in figure 2

Second, let's consider overlap. A quick glance at Figure 21 shows that overlap in a heavy-air genoa restricts traveler movement unless one is willing to accept severe backwind in the mainsail and a closed-up slot. No movement of the traveler results in excessive heeling due to the force exerted by the mainsail. Obviously neither situation is desirable.

The really important factor comes to light when we consider the actual shape of a wide low genoa in heavy air. This is shown by the dotted line in Figure 21 and is exaggerated for clarity. As you can see, the point of maximum camber moves aft, resulting in less forward drive, more drag, increased backwind in the mainsail, and finally a far greater heeling moment. It is obvious that the wider a sail is made, the more cloth there is to stretch on the bias, and the more aggravated this condition becomes.

Finally, add to this the fact that sail interaction, or slot effect, decreases drastically in importance as a boat is overpowered.

What is the answer to all this? Simple! Figure 22 shows the effect of less overlap. By moving the clew forward there are no traveler or backwind problems.

Fig. 23

F_T = Total Force
F_F = Forward Force
F_S = Sideways Force

Yacht Centerline

There is less stretch, because the sail is narrow, and the sail has a better windward shape with less heeling moment and a desirable amount of sail interaction.

Last we have luff length. Figure 23 shows a section of a well-shaped genoa. By vector analysis or simple eyeball, it is obvious that the forward thrust of any sail comes from the forward one third or luff area. It stands to reason then that by shortening the luff we reduce the amount of horsepower pushing us ahead.

Furthermore, that portion which so many people are prone to cut off is, because of its height, in the area of maximum wind velocity and probably the most effective part of the entire sail. In most cases, when these sails are used, sea conditions are proportionately bad and we need more power, not less, to maintain our speed.

In addition, the lower part of the sail is in the lee of the seas when in a trough and its effectiveness is further decreased. The old argument that a higher sail has a higher center of effort and therefore more heeling effect is somewhat true. However, the case against the lower, fatter sail is far more condemning.

What then should a proper #2 and #3 look like? Well this depends on a number of variables starting with the type of boat, ending with the area you intend to sail in, and encompassing a great deal in between. Figure 24 clearly demonstrates the principle of reducing area by reducing overlap, and this is the key to better heavy air genoas.

Fig. 24

Appendix D

How to get ahead going upwind: Winning means maxi-tack

(First published as a feature in *SAIL* magazine.)

There are many sailors around who can sail their boats quite well on an overall basis. But when it comes to going to windward they usually get skunked. I was talking this problem over with a skipper who was convinced that his trouble was that he tacked too much on the windward leg. I suggested that he probably tacked too little. We finally both sat down and did some arithmetic on windshifts and their effect on a boat sailing to windward. The results were astonishing.

FIGURE 1

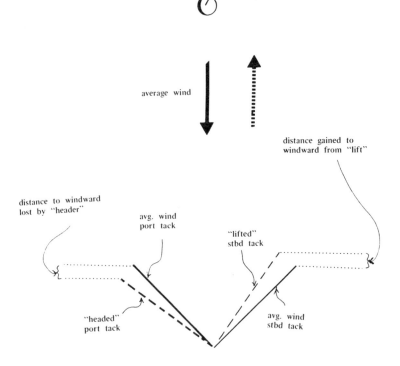

average wind

distance gained to
windward from "lift"

distance to windward
lost by "header"

avg. wind
port tack

"lifted"
stbd tack

"headed"
port tack

avg. wind
stbd tack

When we asked some more friends we found that they too had mistaken ideas about what it is worth to tack when you are headed. The answer seems to be that practically no one tacks as quickly or as often as he should. And that is why the "hot shots" pull out in front on a beat.

In a small centerboarder you should probably tack *whenever you are headed*—period. The cost of making the tack is so slight compared to the cost of being on the wrong tack for only as much as 10 or 20 seconds that you should tack on every detectable header.

In a heavier boat the header will have to last for maybe 30 seconds to compensate for time lost tacking. If it lasts longer you will be ahead of the game from that point on.

These conclusions are general, of course, applying to windshifts of around 10 degrees and to boats that can be tacked without extraordinary loss of time and distance. Obviously, the size of a windshift affects the "payback" time, as does the cost of tacking. And, of course, there'll be times when tactical considerations such as nearby boats, obstructions, or a competitor you want to cover will outweigh the immediate need to go fast upwind.

In such cases you won't tack because you have a good reason not to. But it still is useful for you to keep in mind two key sets of figures:

First—know how much it's worth to be on the lifted tack instead of the headed tack.

Second—know the average time-to-payback, which answers the question how long must a shift hold to get back the distance/time lost tacking on the header.

It's worth more to be on the *lifted tack* than most people realize. The reason probably is that one thinks about only half the problem; when you're headed, you only think about the few degrees your course has fallen off. You *fail* to think of the equal number of degrees the fellow on the other tack is being lifted.

Only a 5-degree wind shift (which is about as small a shift as most skippers will notice) is worth 10 degrees difference between a boat on the headed tack and one on the lifted tack. (See Figure 1.)

With a 5-degree shift, the boat on the lifted tack gains

about four lengths' "lift" to windward after 50 lengths of sailing. That's 8 percent! And at the same time, a boat on the opposite tack *loses* four lengths. That's also 8 percent, or a total of 16 percent difference between the two boats!

This means that if the boats had started out even, and the shift lasted *only* the 50 lengths sailing time (around two minutes or so, in many racing boat classes), the boat on the lifted tack would be about *eight lengths* ahead when next they met. Not bad for a couple of minutes sailing.

The advantage of the lifted tack over the headed tack varies almost directly with the size of the wind shift. If the wind shift is 10 degrees, the advantage of the lifted tack becomes about 31 percent; for a 20-degree shift it's an astounding 58 percent, which is to say that in such a shift you gain or lose a length on your opposite tack opponent with every two lengths sailed! A heading windshift doesn't have to last very long to make it pay to get yourself on the lifted tack.

What does it cost to tack? Of course there may be some independent considerations, such as a gained or lost opportunity to cover an opponent, and there may be local constraints such as obstructions. And you can't ignore wear and tear on people and gear that are also associated with the maneuver. But if you and your boat are in proper condition for racing, you should be able to stand all the tacking it takes to win.

In the smallest classes, the cost of making a smooth tack in good conditions shouldn't be more than about half a boat length of sailing distance, after considering the distance the boat "shoots" to windward, the loss of speed, and the time required to regain speed.

In larger boats, the cost will be two or three times as much, and can range up to as much as about five lengths of sailing for very heavy boats. Bad sailing conditions (very light airs or very rough water) can easily double these values. Extreme conditions can make the cost of tacking even greater.

In very light airs and true drifting weather, whatever momentum you may have is invaluable, of course. Forget about making extra tacks except when it's simply unavoidable.

Once you have a feel for what the cost for a tack is in

time and distance for both you and your boat, you have what it needs to calculate how long a shift has to last to pay you back for tacking on the header. Since you're probably like me and resist doing arithmetic, you'll find it's most convenient to get a feel for the values in a table like the one I have developed above.

Key values in the table are the percentages of relative advantage to the lifted tack vs. the headed tack, shown in Figure 1—16 percent for a 5-degree shift, 31 percent for a 10-degree shift, and 58 percent for a 20-degree shift. Using these figures, if you know how much time it costs you to tack, you can figure exactly how long the shift must last to pay you back for the tack. For example, if a tack costs you five seconds, and being on the other right tack is worth 31 percent, then you'll pay back the tack in 5 ÷ .31 or 16 seconds, and from that point on will start profiting.

To convert an estimate of the cost of tacking (expressed in terms of lengths of sailing distance to sailing time), you will be in the right neighborhood if you use two seconds per length for small, light boats, three seconds per length for small keelboats (up to 25 feet), and five seconds for large offshore hulls.

This leads most skippers to values of five seconds per tack in a very light boat, with the best case going as low as one second, the worst case not much over ten seconds. A medium-size boat will most commonly figure about 10 to 15 seconds sailing, and offshore types will range 20 to 30 seconds sailing. These are values for sailing good conditions. Double them for light air or rough water. (Halve the values for "hot" boats like an E22, Tempest, and FD.)

You now have what it takes to construct a table.

TIME TO PAY BACK COST OF TACK

Cost of Tack	Amount of Wind Shift in Degrees			
	5°	10°	15°	20°
1 sec.	7 secs.	3 secs.	2½ secs.	2 secs.
2 secs.	13 secs.	6½ secs.	4½ secs.	3½ secs.
5 secs.	31 secs.	16 secs.	11½ secs.	8½ secs.
10 secs.	62 secs.	32 secs.	23 secs.	17 secs.
20 secs.	125 secs.	65 secs.	45 secs.	35 secs.
30 secs.	188 secs.	97 secs.	68 secs.	52 secs.

To use the table a 420 skipper, for instance, with a two-second cost of tacking, would see that he begins to gain after only about six or seven seconds on a 10-degree wind shift.

My conclusion is that a light boat should invariably tack on *every* noticeable header unless there's a tactical reason that he can't or unless it's the flukiest of flukey days. Heavier boats can afford to think twice on very slight shifts and wait to see if they'll hold. But even they can't afford to sit around very long on them, and they certainly ought to tack on radical shifts.

Most of us don't tack as readily as we should either because we fail to appreciate quite how much is gained or lost by being on shifts, because we're simply too lazy to make the tacks, or because we don't notice the shifts.

Don't let a shift sneak in one degree at a time without noticing it. If you don't sail by a compass, be sure to eyeball some kind of bearing (if you can) every time you tack. If you find you're no longer able to fetch that bearing you know you've been headed.

I suspect the relative advantage of the lifted tack over the headed tack is much greater than most people realize. And those of you who think that every wind shift is balanced by one in the other direction (and if you just wait a couple of minutes you'll probably get a compensating lift), well, keep on thinking that if you like. Me, I'll tack on both headers and ride the lifted tack both ways!

Maxi-tack and covering

Many top skippers dislike the idea of maxi-tacking because they feel that this diverts them from an even more important mission: covering a trailing opponent. It's axiomatic among racing skippers that they should "cover" major opponents, once in front of them. This is usually understood to mean staying between the opponent and the next mark, and always staying on the same tack as the covered opponent. Obviously, you can't maxi-tack without generally violating that "stay on the same tack" rule of covering.

Actually, it's quite possible to meet the objective of covering an opponent without giving up the benefits of maxi-tacking. This is done *by sailing within a general-coverage area,* described below. At any time that the wind is at or near

FIGURE 2

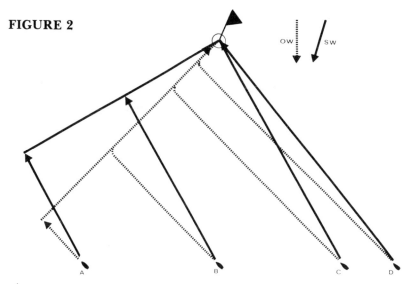

Under the original wind (OW), points A,B,C, & D were all the same sailing distance from the mark (dotted lines). With the shifted wind (SW), the sailing courses are those shown with solid lines, which are not equal:

A is 107% of the old sailing distance
B is 95%
C is 80%— the ideal position
for this windshift, as
C can now exactly
fetch the mark
D is 89%— able to more than
fetch the mark, as
if overstood.

(A prudent skipper in position D would probably sail a course to the right of the direct line for part of the distance, "banking" some windward distance against the possibility of another windshift to the left (counter-clockwise).

the average, and there is no maxi-tack determination as to a lifted tack, sail on the tack of your choice which best serves to position you in that area. As long as you are in the area, whenever there's a usable wind shift, maxi-tack (sail always on the lifted tack); sail on the headed tack only when it's necessary to reenter the general-coverage area.

Figure 2 shows that, with a wind shift to the right (clockwise), boats on the right side of the course generally fare better than those on the left of the course centerline. Boats far to the left are exposed to badly overstanding the mark, causing a substantial loss of position relative to boats farther to the right of the course. Boats that are far to the right of the course may find that they are lifted so far as to fetch the mark immediately—if they have something to spare (that is, can more than fetch the course mark), they, too will have potentially overstood, but not so disastrously as those to the left of the course, for these boats merely free their sheets a bit, and sailing a bit faster than close-hauled make out quite well.

The obvious conclusion (ignoring other boats for the moment) is that the skipper who plans to optimize the use of wind shifts by maxi-tacking—that is, tacking on every apparent header to sail always on the tack that makes most ground toward the mark—should *keep to a course* more or less *near the centerline* of the course. Assuming random shifts of the wind to right and left of the average wind, he is then in position to enjoy the benefits of temporary lifts, without great exposure to being left out beyond the average wind's layline, as happens to boat "A" in Figure 2.

When you feel inspired with insight as to the direction of the coming shift, sail "toward the new wind"—that is, to the right of the course centerline if you expect a shift to the right, and to the left of the course if the shift will be to the left.

The ideal position would be to sail just far enough to the side of the course to be able to fetch the mark when the wind shifts. (Boat "C" in Figure 2 is in that position.)

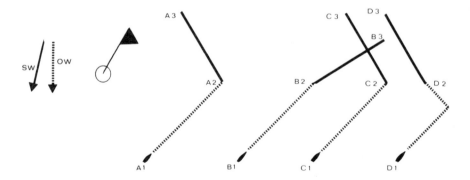

FIGURE 3

Sailing under the original wind (OW), the distance to sail to the mark would be the same for A,B,C, & D (position 1). At position 2 there is a temporary wind shift (SW). Boats at A2 and C2 are headed and tack immediately; boat at D2 is lifted; boat at B2 continues to sail, headed. After two minutes' sailing the windshift ends, returning to direction OW. Boats at A3, C3, and D3 are again even; boat at B3 is clearly behind.

The next point to understand is that while there is great advantage in maxi-tacking (sailing always on the lifted tack, never on the headed one), the advantages are the same for all boats without regard to their position to right or left of the course centerline *provided the windshift is temporary.* In Figure 2 it was assumed that the shifted wind held until all boats reached the mark; in that case (a clockwise shift), boats to the right of the course gained over boats on the left. Now, Figure 3 shows that with a temporary shift, all boats sailing on the lifted tack hold their relative positions. By way of contrast, boat "X" in Figure 3 is shown sailing on the headed tack—with a substantial loss of distance relative to boats "W," "Y," and "Z."

A summary, then, of what wind shifts will do to you (without considering other boats) would be:

If the shift does not hold long enough for boats to reach the layline (either the average wind's layline or the current shift's layline), *all boats that get the shift are equally helped.* (Or, equally hindered if they sail on the headed tack.)

If the shift holds long enough for boats to reach the layline, *some will be helped* relative to others, depending upon their position to right or left of the course centerline. When the wind shifts to the right, boats to the right gain more; when the wind shifts to the left, boats to the left gain; it is possible to be too far to the left or right if you can more than fetch the mark with the new shift.

Now, let's consider what the best strategy for covering would be. With regard to any one boat that's behind you, there are only three different ways in which you might be affected by a wind shift:

1. you get a shift that he does not get;
2. you both get a shift; or
3. he gets a wind shift that you do not get.

Case 1—only you get it. If the shift is a lift, you laugh quietly to yourself and get farther ahead. If the shift is a header, you "maxi-tack"—thus turning it into a lift—and get farther ahead. Either way you gain, and your only concern

is whether or not you're sailing so far away from your opponent as to risk losing the cover.

Case 2—you both get it. If it's a lift because you're already
on the favored tack, you enjoy it; if it's a header, maxi-tack.
As before, your relative position won't be hurt . . . and it
can improve if your opponent stays on the headed tack.

Case 3—only your following opponent gets it. (If he
doesn't understand the principles behind "maxi-tack," and
sails on the headed tack, you get another chance to smile
quietly as you lengthen your lead.) We need to consider
only the cases in which your opponent sails the lifted tack.
In such cases, he will close some of the gap between
you—that's inevitable. What you can do is to sail for a position such that he cannot sail past you.

FIGURE 4

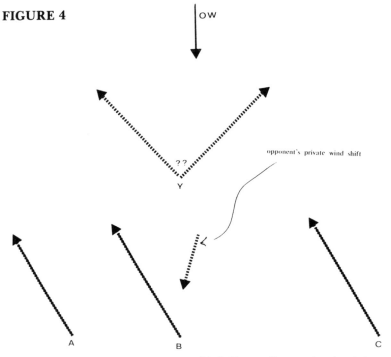

At position Y you can see opponent getting lifted. If you sail on starboard tack (toward
the left side of the course) opponent in position A or B cannot pass, as his course must
meet your tack — at which point either his private wind shift must end, or you must share
it. But from position C you must go onto the opposite tack to cover the opponent, so that
your track will cross his.

Look at Figure 4. If you were in position "Y" when you noticed your following opponent getting lifted, you would have the opportunity to choose between the illustrated starboard and port tack courses. It becomes clear that an opponent in position B or C could not expect to pass you if you sailed on port tack—his lifted course would have to converge with yours, and sooner or later he must sail into your "average wind," or you must get to share his private lifting wind shift. When that occurs, his advantage disappears, and he no longer threatens to pass you (although he is then closer than before he got the lift).

In position A, the following opponent could in fact sail past you if you were on the same (port) tack. If his lift were to hold, and you never got it, he could end up well ahead of you owing to the better angle of sailing. Your move is obvious: sail on the starboard tack until you have crossed his track and are upwind of him; you should then resume covering on the same track, when he is placed in a position comparable to those of B and C (converging course from leeward).

A summary of positional relationships would be:

You shouldn't be passed by a following opponent whose track converges with yours; you might be passed by an opponent whose track (when lifted) goes to windward of your wake.

To insure keeping ahead of your opponent, sail for a position that is upwind of his course; an opponent who is behind but to windward is dangerous, but one who is ahead but to leeward is "covered."

Summary: with only one opponent—or only one that you care much about for this race—try to stay between him and the mark. Doing so assures that any private wind shift he gets will put him onto a course with which you can converge from windward.

With one or many opponents, stay as close to the centerline of the course as is practical, so as to have the best probability of being helped by wind shifts.

Maxi-tack to assure that you sail on the lifted tack in temporary wind shifts.

An optimizing approach to meet all three of these objectives moderately well is this: think of a pie-shaped area on the water which is bounded on one side by the line from the mark to your opponent, and on the other side by the centerline of the course. (See Figure 5.) As long as you sail roughly within this area, you should be free to maxi-tack without danger of being carried off to a disastrous position or losing your covered opponent.

FIGURE 5

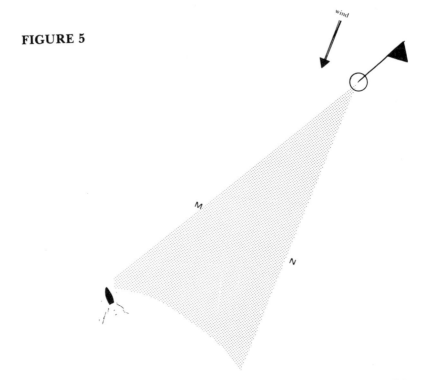

You can maxi-tack while maintaining cover so long as you sail in the shaded area bounded by M (line from mark to opponent) and N (centerline of course).

If you must choose between covering one opponent who is nearest you but splitting away from the fleet, or covering the majority who are following similar courses, I believe the best strategy is : *cover the most, not the nearest.*

The wind isn't always blowing on a "shift"; sometimes it blows "down the middle"—that's the time to choose the best tack for getting back into position. Good position is worth more than the cost of one tack.

Appendix E

How much favored *is* "the favored end of the line"?

(First published as a feature in *SAIL* magazine.)

A normal starting line should be at right angles to the wind, with the first mark directly upwind from the line. In such a case, the trip to the first mark is exactly the same distance no matter where on the line you start. (See Figure 1.)

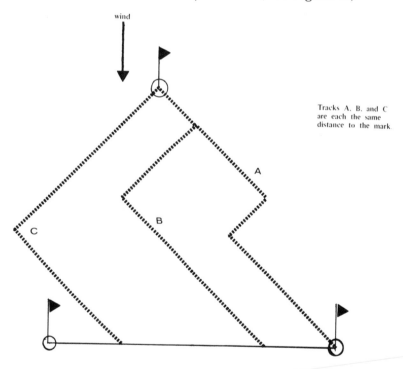

wind

Tracks A. B. and C
are each the same
distance to the mark

FIGURE 1

With such an even line (square to the wind), there will be a tactical advantage for boats starting at the right-hand end of the line: they will have freedom to tack onto port tack whenever they choose, whereas left-end starters will have to wait until the fleet spreads out somewhat before they have room to go onto port tack without having to face a dangerous passage through a bunch of right-of-way starboard tackers.

Because of this advantage at the right end, many race committees like to tip the line a little (5 to 10 degrees is usual) in order to "favor" the other end, hopefully spreading the fleet away from the right-hand corner of the line.

Other reasons may lead to a line with a favored end—local traffic patterns, obstructions, shifting winds, or lazy race committees may produce lines not laid out at right angles to the wind.

A "favored" end will be closer to where you want to go than the other end. Figure 2 shows this difference. Using a sheet of graph paper makes it easy to see how far it is from several assumed starting lines. This drawing illustrates that shifting the line 10 degrees off normal produces a distance saving of 26 percent of the length of the line. Similarly, shifting the line 30 degrees off normal produces a distance saving of 70 percent of the length of the line. (That is, if the line were around 20 lengths long, the favored end would be about 14 lengths closer to the mark than the other end! That's a very considerable distance in any kind of close competition.

The suggested conclusion is, that while it isn't worth cramming into a messy crowd of boats to get to the very end of a favored line, you shouldn't go very far from that corner. Giving up a few lengths' distance from the favored corner is likely to be a good exchange if it buys you clear air and room to start at top speed—but don't go any farther than absolutely necessary.

Measuring the favored end before the start is most simply done by crossing the line, luffing head to wind. (See Figure 3.) Whichever end of the line you're pointing toward is favored. You can easily estimate about how far it is off normal by judging the angle the line makes with the beam of the boat.

Speaking of favored lines, try not to be confused by a windward mark that is not directly upwind of the line. The fact that the first mark is somewhat to right or left of the center of the line, looking dead upwind, *makes no difference*

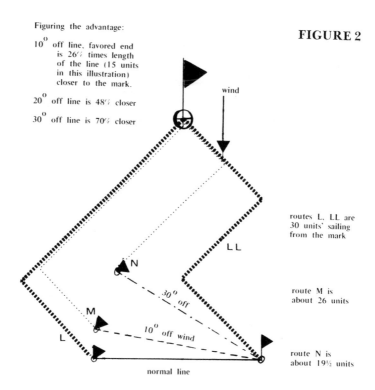

Figuring the advantage:

10° off line, favored end is 26% times length of the line (15 units in this illustration) closer to the mark.

20° off line is 48% closer

30° off line is 70% closer

FIGURE 2

wind

routes L, LL are 30 units' sailing from the mark

LL

route M is about 26 units

N

30° off

M

10° off wind

L

route N is about 19½ units

normal line

at all, provided only that at least one tack is still necessary to reach the mark.

I know this flies in the teeth of all you've been taught, but figure it out. You'll quickly see that the distance is always the same, no matter where you start and no matter how many tacks you make. (However, making many tacks may be slower than making only a few, depending upon how much speed and time you lose on each tack in your boat, and on your success with "maxi-tack" wind shifts.)

On any off-the-wind start, where you don't have to tack, whether it's down wind, reaching, or something you can fetch close-hauled, there is a slight advantage in starting at the end that is closest to the mark. But other things count more. They are finding clean air and room to maneuver. And, if the mark is not far enough away to separate the fleet, it's important to start at the end of the line that will put you inside with buoy room rights when turning at the first mark.

Keep in mind the distance saved to the mark when there's a favored end of the line. When the line is tilted more than about five degrees, you *must* start as near the favored end as you possibly can. If it's tilted more than 10 or 15 degrees, it will be worth getting into a couple of boat lengths' worth of hassle with the fleet in order to be near the right end. You shouldn't mix it up with the thickest part of the fleet though—it will be disastrous! You can usually find a spot about three lengths in from the corner that is not too crowded.

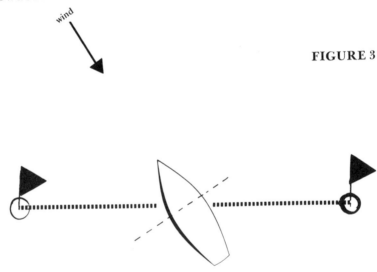

FIGURE 3

Luffing head-to-wind bow points toward favored left end. Angle from abeam to line shows how much off line is.

Appendix F

Racing Rules

Sailboats throughout the world race under the same code of rules, administered by the International Yacht Racing Union (IYRU); these are in turn distributed by local authorities. In the United States and Canada, the governing body is the North American Yacht Racing Union (NAYRU). All of the rules about right-of-way, which are found in Section IV of the rule book, are the same as those issued by IYRU, as are most of the other rules governing the management of races—although a few of the finer points in these other sections of the rule book may vary in details from the IYRU version or those of other national authorities.

The current edition of the official NAYRU Rules is reproduced below.

Part I—Definitions

When a term defined in Part I is used in its defined sense it is printed in **bold** *type. All definitions and italicized notes rank as rules.*

Racing—A yacht is **racing** from her preparatory signal until she has either **finished** and cleared the finishing line and finishing **marks** or retired, or until the race has been **cancelled, postponed** or **abandoned**, except that in match or team races, the sailing instructions may prescribe that a yacht is **racing** from any specified time before the preparatory signal.

Starting—A yacht **starts** when, after fulfilling her penalty obligations, if any, under rule 51.1(*c*), Sailing the Course, and after her starting signal, any part of her hull, crew or equipment first crosses the starting line in the direction of the course to the first **mark**.

Finishing—A yacht **finishes** when any part of her hull, or of her crew or equipment in normal position, crosses the finishing line from the direction of the course from the last **mark**, after fulfilling her penalty obligations, if any, under rule 52.2, Touching a Mark.

Luffing—Altering course towards the wind until head to wind.

Tacking—A yacht is **tacking** from the moment she is beyond head to wind until she has **borne away**, if beating to windward, to a **close-hauled** course; if not beating to windward, to the course on which her mainsail has filled.

Bearing Away—Altering course away from the wind until a yacht begins to **jibe**.

Jibing—A yacht begins to **jibe** at the moment when, with the wind aft, the foot of her mainsail crosses her centre line and completes the **jibe** when the mainsail has filled on the other **tack**.

On a Tack—A yacht is **on a tack** except when she is **tacking** or **jibing**. A yacht is on the **tack (starboard** or **port)** corresponding to her **windward** side.

Close-hauled—A yacht is **close-hauled** when sailing by the wind as close as she can lie with advantage in working to windward.

Clear Astern and **Clear Ahead; Overlap**—A yacht is **clear astern** of another when her hull and equipment in normal position are abaft an imaginary line projected abeam from the aftermost point of the other's hull and equipment in normal position. The other yacht is **clear ahead**. The yachts **overlap** if neither is **clear astern**; or if, although one is **clear astern**, an intervening yacht **overlaps** both of them. The terms **clear astern, clear ahead** and **overlap** apply to yachts on opposite **tacks** only when they are subject to rule 42, Rounding or Passing Marks and Obstructions.

Leeward and **Windward**—The **leeward** side of a yacht is that on which she is, or, if **luffing** head to wind, was, carrying her mainsail. The opposite side is the **windward** side.

When neither of two yachts on the same **tack** is **clear astern**, the one on the **leeward** side of the other is the **leeward yacht**. The other is the **windward yacht**.

Proper course—A **proper course** is any course which a yacht might sail after the starting signal, in the absence of the other yacht or yachts affected, to **finish** as quickly as possible. The course sailed before **luffing** or **bearing away** is presumably, but not necessarily, that yacht's **proper course**. There is no **proper course** before the starting signal.

Mark—A **mark** is any object specified in the sailing instructions which a yacht must round or pass on a required side.

Every ordinary part of a **mark** ranks as part of it, including a flag, flagpole, boom or hoisted boat, but excluding ground tackle and any object either accidentally or temporarily attached to the **mark**.

Obstruction—An **obstruction** is any object, including craft under way, large enough to require a yacht, if not less than one overall length away from it, to make a substantial alteration of course to pass on one side or the other, or any object which can be passed on one side only, including a buoy when the yacht in question cannot safely pass between it and the shoal or object which it marks.

Cancellation—A **cancelled** race is one which the race committee decides will not be sailed thereafter.

Postponement—A **postponed** race is one which is not started at its scheduled time and which can be sailed at any time the race committee may decide.

Abandonment—An **abandoned** race is one which the race committee declares void at any time after the starting signal, and which can be re-sailed at its discretion.

Part II—Management of Races

Authority and Duties of Race Committee: *The rules of Part II deal with the duties and responsibilities of the Race Committee in conducting a race, the meaning of signals made by it and of other actions taken by it.*

1—General Authority of Race Committee and Jury or Judges

1. All races shall be arranged, conducted and judged by a Race Committee under the direction of the sponsoring organization, except as may be provided under rule 1.2. The Race Committee may delegate the conduct of a race, the hearing and deciding of protests or any other of its responsibilities to one or more sub-committees which, if appointed, will hereinafter be included in the term "Race Committee" wherever it is used.

2. For a special regatta or series, the sponsoring organization may provide for a Jury or Judges to hear and decide protests and to have supervision over the conduct of the races, in which case the Race Committee shall be subject to the direction of the Jury or Judges to the extent provided by the sponsoring organization.

3. All yachts entered or **racing** shall be subject to the direction and control of the Race Committee, but it shall be the sole responsibility of each yacht to decide whether or not to **start** or to continue to **race**.

4. The Race Committee may reject any entry without stating the reason.

However, at all world and continental championships, no entry within established quotas shall be rejected without first obtaining the approval of the I.Y.R.U. or the duly authorized international class association.

5. The Race Committee shall be governed by these rules, by the prescriptions of its National Authority, by the sailing instructions, by approved class rules (but it may refuse to recognize any class rule which conflicts with these rules) and, when applicable, by the international team racing rules, and shall decide all questions in accordance therewith.

2—Notice of Race
The notice of a race or regatta shall contain the following information:—

(*a*) That the race or races will be sailed under the rules of the I.Y.R.U., the prescriptions of the national authority and the rules of each class concerned.

(*b*) The date and place of the regatta and the time of the start of the first race and, if possible, succeeding races.

(*c*) The class or classes for which races will be given.

The notice shall also cover such of the following matters as may be appropriate:—

(*d*) Any special instructions, subject to rule 3.1, which may vary or add to these rules or class rules.

(*e*) Any restrictions or conditions regarding entries and numbers of starters or competitors.

(*f*) The address to which entries shall be sent, the date on which they close, the amount of entrance fees, if any, and any other entry requirements.

(*g*) Particulars and number of prizes.

(*h*) Time and place for receiving sailing instructions.

(*i*) Scoring system.

(*j*) That for the purpose of determining the result of a race which is one of a series of races in a competition, decisions of protests shall not be subject to appeal if it is essential to establish the results promptly.

3—The Sailing Instructions

1. **Status**—These rules shall be supplemented by written sailing instructions which shall rank as rules and may alter a rule by specific reference to it, but except in accordance with rule 3.2 (*b*) (ii) they shall not alter Parts I and IV of these rules; provided however, that this restriction shall not preclude the right of developing and testing proposed rule changes in local regattas.

2. **Contents**—(*a*) The sailing instructions shall contain the following information:—

(i) That the race or races will be sailed under the rules of the I.Y.R.U., the prescriptions of the National Authority, the sailing instructions and the rules of each class concerned.

(ii) The course or courses to be sailed or a list of **marks** or courses from which the course or courses will be selected, describing all **marks** and stating the order in which and the side on which each is to be rounded or passed.

(iii) The course signals.

(iv) The classes to race and class signals, if any.

(v) Time of start for each class.

(vi) Starting line and starting area if used.

(vii) Finishing line and any special instructions for shortening the course or for **finishing** a shortened course. (Where possible it is good practice for the sailing instructions for **finishing** a shortened course not to differ from those laid down for **finishing** the full course.)

(viii) Time limit, if any, for **finishing**.

(ix) Scoring system, if not previously announced in writing, including the method, if any, for breaking ties.

(*b*) The sailing instructions shall also cover such of the following matters as may be appropriate:—

(i) The date and place of the race or races.

(ii) When the race is to continue after sunset, the time or place, if any, at which the International Regulations for Preventing Collisions at Sea, or Government Right-of-Way Rules, shall replace the corresponding rules of Part IV, and the night signals the committee boat will display.

(iii) Any special instructions, subject to rule 3.1, which may vary or add to these rules, or class rules, and any special signals.

(iv) Eligibility; entry; measurement certificate; declaration.

(v) Any special instruction or signal, if any, regarding the carrying on board and wearing of personal buoyancy.

(vi) Names, national letters and distinguishing numbers and ratings, if any, of the yachts entered.

(vii) Any special instructions governing the methods of starting and recall.

(viii) Recall numbers or letters, if used, of the yachts entered.

(ix) Time allowances.

(x) Length of course or courses.

(xi) Method by which competitors will be notified of any change of course.

(xii) Information on tides and currents.

(xiii) Prizes.

(xiv) When rule 68.7, Alternative Penalties, if used, will apply.

(xv) Any special time limit within which, and address at which, a written protest shall be lodged, and the prescribed fee, if any, which shall accompany it.

(xvi) Time and place at which protests will be heard.

(xvii) That for the purpose of determining the result of a race which is one of a series of races in a competition, decisions of protests shall not be subject to appeal if it is essential to establish the results promptly.

(xviii) Whether races **postponed** or **abandoned** for the day will be sailed later and, if so, when and where.

(xix) Disposition to be made of a yacht appearing at the start alone in her class.

(xx) Time and place at which results of races will be posted.

3. **Distribution**—The sailing instructions shall be available to each yacht entitled to race.

4. **Changes**—The Race Committee may change the sailing instructions by notice, in writing if practicable, given to each yacht affected not later than the warning signal of her class.

5. **Oral Instructions**—Oral instructions shall not be given except in accordance with procedure specifically set out in the sailing instructions.

4—Signals

1. **International Code Flag Signals**—Unless otherwise prescribed in the sailing instructions, the following International Code flags shall be used as indicated and when displayed alone they shall apply to all classes, and when displayed over a class signal they shall apply to the designated class only:

"AP", Answering Pennant—Postponement Signal

(*a*) Means:—

"All races not started are **postponed**.

The warning signal will be made one minute after this signal is lowered."

(One sound signal shall be made with the lowering of the "AP".)

(*b*) Over one ball or shape, means:—

"The scheduled starting times of all races not started are **postponed** fifteen minutes."

(This postponement can be extended indefinitely by the addition of one ball or shape for every fifteen minutes.)

(*c*) Over one of the numeral pennants 1 to 9, means:—

"All races not started are **postponed** one hour, two hours, etc."

(*d*) Over the letter "A", means:—

"All races not started are **postponed** to a later date."

"B"—Protest signal.

When displayed by a yacht means:—

"I intend to lodge a protest."

"L"—Means:—
"Come within hail," or "Follow Me."

"M"—Mark Signal.
When displayed on a buoy, vessel, or other object, means:—
"Round or pass the object displaying this signal instead of the **mark** which it replaces."

"N"—Abandonment Signal.
Means:—
"All races are **abandoned**."

"N over X"—Abandonment and Re-sail Signal.
Means:—
"All races are **abandoned** and will shortly be re-sailed. Watch for fresh starting signals."

"N over First Repeater"—Cancellation Signal.
Means:—
"All races are **cancelled**."

"P—Preparatory Signal.
Means:—
"The class designated by the warning signal will **start** in 5 minutes exactly."

"R"—Reverse Course Signal.
Alone, means:—
"Sail the course prescribed in the sailing instructions in the reverse direction."
When displayed over a course signal, means:—
"Sail the designated course in the reverse direction."

"S"—Shorten Course Signal.
(*a*) at or near the starting line, means:—
"Sail the shortened course prescribed in the sailing instructions."
(*b*) at or near the finishing line, means:—
"**Finish** the race either:
(i) at the prescribed finishing line at the end of the round still to be completed by the leading yacht" or

(ii) "in any other manner prescribed in the sailing instructions under rule 3.2 (*a*) (vii)."
(*c*) at or near a rounding **mark**, means:—
"**Finish** between the nearby **mark** and the committee boat."

"1st Repeater"—General Recall Signal.
Means:—
"The class is recalled for a fresh start as provided in sailing instructions."

2. **Signaling the Course**—The Race Committee shall either make the appropriate course signal or otherwise designate the course before or with the warning signal.

3. **Changing the Course**—The course for a class which has not **started** may be changed:—
(*a*) by displaying the appropriate **postponement** signal and indicating the new course before or with the warning signal to be displayed after the lowering of the **postponement** signal; or
(*b*) by displaying a course signal or by removing and substituting a course signal before or with the warning signal.

(Method (*a*) is preferable when a change of course involves either shifting the committee boat or other starting **mark**, or requires a change of sails which cannot reasonably be completed within the five-minute period before the preparatory signal is made.)

4. **Signals for Starting a Race**
(*a*) Unless otherwise prescribed in the sailing instruction, the signals for starting a race shall be made at 5-minute intervals exactly, and shall be either:—
In system (i) when classes are started:—
(a) at ten-minute intervals, the warning signal for each succeeding class shall be broken out or displayed at the starting signal of the preceding class, and
(b) at five-minute intervals, the preparatory signal for the first class to start shall be left flying or displayed until the last class has started. The warning signal for each succeeding class shall be broken out or displayed

at the preparatory signal of the preceding class, or

In system (ii) each signal shall be lowered 30 seconds before the hoisting of the next, and in starting yachts by classes, the starting signal for each class shall be the preparatory signal for the next.

(*b*) Although rule 4.4(*a*) specifies 5-minute intervals between signals, this shall not interfere with the power of a Race Committee to start a series of races at any intervals which it considers desirable.

(*c*) A warning signal shall not be made before its scheduled time, except with the consent of all yachts entitled to race.

(*d*) When a significant error is made in the timing of the interval between any of the signals for starting a race, the recommended procedure is to have a general recall, **abandonment** or **postponement** of the race whose start is directly affected by the error and a corresponding **postponement** of succeeding races. Unless otherwise prescribed in the sailing instructions a new warning signal shall be made. When the race is not recalled, **abandoned** or **postponed** after an error in the timing of the interval, each succeeding signal shall be made at the correct interval from the preceding signal.

5. **Finishing Signals**—Blue flag or shape. When displayed at the finish, means:—"The committee boat is on station at the finishing line."

6. **Other Signals**—The sailing instructions shall designate any other special signals and shall explain their meaning.

7. **Calling Attention to Signals**—Whenever the Race Committee makes a signal, except "R" or "S" before the warning signal, it shall call attention to its action as follows:—

Three guns or other sound signals when displaying "N", "N over X", or "N over 1st Repeater".

Two guns or other sound signals when displaying the "1st Repeater", "AP", or "S".

One gun or other sound signal when making any other signal, including the lowering of "AP" when the length of the postponement is not signalled.

8. **Visual Signal to Govern**—Times shall be taken from the visual starting signals, and a failure or mistiming of a gun or other sound signal shall be disregarded.

5—Cancelling, Postponing or Abandoning a Race and Changing or Shortening Course

1. The Race Committee:—

(*a*) before the starting signal may shorten the course or **cancel** or **postpone** a race for any reason, and

(*b*) after the starting signal may shorten the course by finishing a race at any rounding **mark** or **cancel** or **abandon** a race because of foul weather endangering the yachts, or because of insufficient wind, or because a **mark** is missing or has shifted or for other reasons directly affecting safety or the fairness of the competition.

(*c*) after the starting signal may change the course at any roundir **mark** subject to proper notice being given to each yac it as prescribed in the sailing instructions.

2. After a **postponement** the ordinary starting signals prescribed in rule 4.4(*a*) shall be used, and the postponement signal, if a general one, shall be hauled down before the first warning or course signal is made.

3. The race Committee shall notify all yachts concerned by signal or otherwise when and where a race **postponed** or **abandor d** will be sailed.

6—Starting and Finishing Lines

The starting and finishing lines shall be either:—

(*a*) A line between a **mark** and a mast or staff on the committee boat or station clearly identified in the sailing instructions;

(*b*) a line between two **marks**; or

(*c*) the extension of a line through two stationary posts, with or without a **mark** at or near its outer limit, inside which the yachts shall pass.

For types (*a*) and (*c*) of starting or finishing lines the sailing instructions may also prescribe that a **mark** will be laid at or near the inner end of the line, in which case yachts shall pass between it and the outer **mark**.

7—Start of a Race

1. **Starting Area**—The sailing instructions may define a starting area which may be bounded by buoys; if so, they shall not rank as **marks**.

2. **Timing the Start**—The start of a yacht shall be timed from her starting signal.

8—Recalls

1. Yachts' sail numbers shall be used as recall numbers except that the Race Committee may instead allot a suitable recall number or letter to each yacht in accordance with rule 3.2(b) (viii).

2. When, at her starting signal, any part of a yacht's hull, crew or equipment is on the course side of the starting line or its extensions, or she is subject to rule 51.1(c), Sailing the Course, the Race Committee shall:

(a) when each yacht has been allotted a recall number or letter, display her recall number or letter as soon as possible and make a suitable sound signal. As soon as the recalled yacht has wholly returned to the pre-start side of the line or its extensions, the Race Committee shall so inform her by removing her recall number or letter. This is the preferred procedure.

(b) When no recall number or letter has been alotted, make a sound signal and leave the class warning signal at "the dip" or display such other signal as may be prescribed in the sailing instructions, until she has wholly returned to the pre-start side of the line or its extensions, or for such shorter period as the Race Committee considers reasonable.

The responsibility for returning shall rest with the yacht concerned.

(c) Follow such other procedure as may be prescribed in the sailing instructions.

3. (a) When there is either a number of unidentified premature starters, or an error in starting procedure, the Race Committee may make a general recall signal in accordance with rules 4.1, "First Repeater", and 4.7, Calling Attention to Signals. Unless otherwise prescribed in

the sailing instructions, new warning and preparatory signals shall be made.

(*b*) Except as provided in rule 31.2, Disqualification, rule infringements before the preparatory signal for the new start shall be disregarded for the purpose of starting in the race to be re-started.

9—Marks

1. Mark Missing

(*a*) When any **mark** either is missing or has shifted, the Race Committee shall, if possible, replace it in its stated position, or substitute a new one with similar characteristics or a buoy or vessel displaying the letter "M" of the International Code—the **mark** signal.

(*b*) If it is impossible either to replace the **mark** or to substitute a new one in time for the yachts to round or pass it, the Race Committee may, at its discretion, act in accordance with rule 5.1, Cancelling, Postponing or Abandoning a Race and Changing or Shortening Course.

2. **Mark Unseen**—When races are sailed in fog or at night, dead reckoning alone should not necessarily be accepted as evidence that a **mark** has been rounded or passed.

10—Finishing Within a Time Limit

Unless otherwise prescribed in the sailing instructions, in races where there is a time limit, one yacht **finishing** within the prescribed limit shall make the race valid for all other yachts in that race.

11—Ties

When there is a tie at the finish of a race, either actual or on corrected times, the points for the place for which the yachts have tied and for the place immediately below shall be added together and divided equally. When two or more yachts tie for a trophy or prize in either a single race or a series, the yachts so tied shall, if practicable, sail a deciding race; if not, either the tie shall be broken by a method established under rule 3.2 (*a*) (ix), or the yachts so tied shall either receive equal prizes or share the prize.

12—Yacht Materially Prejudiced

When, upon the request of a yacht made within the time limit provided by rule 68.3 (*e*), Protests, or when the Race Committee, upon its own initiative, decides that, through no fault of her own, the finishing position of a yacht has been materially prejudiced: by rendering assistance in accordance with rule 58, Rendering Assistance; by being disabled by another yacht which was required to keep clear; or by an action or omission of the Race Committee; it may **cancel** or **abandon** the race or make such other arrangement as it deems equitable.

13—Races to be Re-sailed

When a race is to be re-sailed:—
    1. All yachts entered in the original race shall be eligible to **start** in the race to be re-sailed.
    2. Subject to the entry requirements of the original race, and at the discretion of the Race Committee, new entries may be accepted.
    3. Rule infringements in the original race shall be disregarded for the purpose of **starting** in the race to be re-sailed.
    4. The Race Committee shall notify the yachts concerned when and where the race will be re-sailed.

14—Award of Prizes, Places and Points

    1. Before awarding the prizes, the Race Committee shall be satisfied that all yachts whose finishing positions affect the awards have observed the racing rules, the prescriptions of the National Authority, the sailing instructions and the class rules.

2. The sailing instructions may prescribe that in a particular instance the Race Committee may require the member in charge of a yacht to submit within a stated time limit a signed declaration to the effect that "all the racing rules, the prescriptions of the National Authority, the sailing instructions and the class rules were observed in the race (or races) on (date or dates of race or races)." A yacht which fails to observe the above requirement may, at the discretion of the Race Committee, be disqualified, or regarded as having retired.

(Numbers 15, 16 and 17 are spare numbers.)

Part III—General Requirements

Owner's Responsibilities for Qualifying his Yacht: *A yacht intending to* **race** *shall, to avoid subsequent disqualification, comply with the rules of Part III before her preparatory signal and, when applicable, while* **racing**.

18—Entries

Entries shall be made as required by the notice of the race or by the sailing instructions.

19—Measurement Certificates

1. Every yacht entering a race shall hold such valid measurement or rating certificate as may be required by the National Authority or other duly authorized body, by her class rules, by the notice of the race, or by the sailing instructions.

2. It shall be the owner's responsibility to maintain his yacht in the condition upon which her certificate was based.

3. (*a*) If the owner of a yacht cannot produce such a certificate when required, he may be permitted to sign and lodge with the Race Committee, before she **starts**, a statement in the following form:

To the Secretary . . . . Club
UNDERTAKING TO PRODUCE CERTIFICATE
The yacht. . . . . competes in
the . . . . race on condition that a valid certificate pre-
viously issued by the authorized administrative body, or a true
copy of it, is submitted to the Race Committee before the end
of the series, and that she competes in the race(s) on the measure-
ment or rating of that certificate.
Signed . . . .
(Owner or his representative)
Date . . . .
(b) In this event the sailing instructions may require that the owner shall lodge such a deposit as may be required by the National Authority, which may be forfeited if such certificate or true copy is not submitted to the Race Committee within the prescribed period.

20—Ownership of Yachts

1. Unless otherwise prescribed in the conditions of entry, a yacht shall be eligible to compete only when she is either owned by or on charter to and has been entered by a yacht or sailing club recognized by a National Authority or a member or members thereof.

2. Two or more yachts owned or chartered wholly or in part by the same body or person shall not compete in the same race without the previous consent of the Race Committee.

21—Member on Board

Every yacht shall have on board a member of a yacht or sailing club recognized by a National Authority to be in charge of the yacht as owner or owner's representative.

22—Shifting Ballast

1. **General Restrictions**. Floorboards shall be kept down; bulkheads and doors left standing; ladders, stairways and water tanks left in place; all cabin, galley and forecastle fix-

tures and fittings kept on board; all movable ballast shall be properly stowed under the floorboards or in lockers and no dead weight shall be shifted.

2. **Shipping, Unshipping or Shifting Ballast; Water**. No ballast, whether movable or fixed, shall be shipped, unshipped or shifted, nor shall any water be taken in or discharged except for ordinary ship's use, from 2100 hours on the day before the race until the yacht is no longer **racing**, except that bilge water may be removed at any time.

3. **Clothing and Equipment**.

(a) A competitor shall not wear or carry any clothing or equipment for the purpose of increasing his weight.

(b) A class which desires to make exception to rule 22.3(a), Clothing and Equipment, may so prescribe in its class rules. In so doing, however, the total weight of clothing and equipment worn or carried by a competitor shall not exceed twenty kilograms when wet.

23—Anchor

Unless otherwise prescribed by her class rules, every yacht shall carry on board an anchor and chain or rope of suitable size.

24—Life-Saving Equipment

Every yacht shall carry life-saving equipment conforming to government regulations for all persons on board, one item of which shall be ready for immediate use.

25—Class Emblems, National Letters and Distinguishing Numbers

1. Every yacht of an international class recognized by the I.Y.R.U. shall carry on her mainsail, or as provided in (d) (iii) and (iv) on her spinnaker:—

(a) An emblem, letter or number denoting the class to which she belongs.

(b) When **racing** in foreign waters a letter or letters showing her nationality, thus:—

A	Argentine	IS	Israel	P	Portugal
AL	Algeria	J	Japan	PH	The
AR	United Arab	K	United		Philippines
	Republic		Kingdom	PK	Pakistan
B	Belgium	KA	Australia	PR	Puerto Rico
BA	Bahamas	KB	Bermuda	PU	Peru
BL	Brazil	KBA	Barbados	PZ	Poland
BU	Bulgaria	KC	Canada	RC	Cuba
CA	Cambodia	KG	Guyana	RI	Indonesia
CB	Colombia	KGB	Gibraltar	RM	Roumania
CY	Republic of	KH	Hong Kong	S	Sweden
	Sri Lanka	KJ	Jamaica	SA	Republic of
CZ	Czechoslovakia	KK	Kenya		South Africa
D	Denmark	KR	Rhodesia	SE	Senegal
DR	Dominican	KS	Singapore	SL	El Salvador
	Republic	KT	Trinidad	SR	Union of
E	Spain		and Tobago		Soviet Socialist
EC	Ecuador	KZ	New Zealand		Republics
F	France	KZA	Zambia	T	Tunisia
G	Federal Re-	L	Finland	TA	Republic of
	public of	LE	Lebanon		China
	Germany	LX	Luxembourg		(Taiwan)
GO	German	M	Hungary	TH	Thailand
	Democratic	MA	Morocco	TK	Turkey
	Republic	MG	Madagascar	U	Uruguay
GR	Greece	MO	Monaco	US	United States
GU	Guatemala	MT	Malta		of America
H	Holland	MX	Mexico	V	Venezuela
HA	Netherland	MY	Malaysia	VI	U.S. Virgin Is.
	Antilles	N	Norway	X	Chile
I	Italy	NK	Democratic	Y	Yugoslavia
IL	Iceland		People's	Z	Switzerland
IND	India		Republic of		
IR	Republic of		Korea		
	Ireland	OE	Austria		

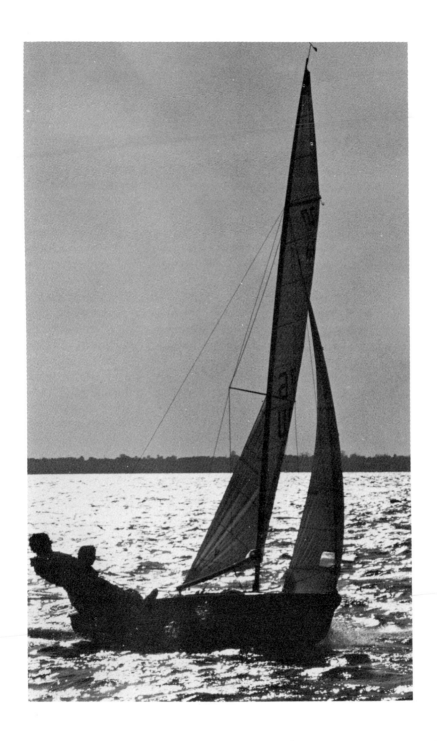

(c) Distinguishing number:—
A distinguishing number allotted to her by her National Authority. In the case of a self-administered international class, the number may be allotted by the class owners' association.
Assuming a Flying Dutchman yacht belonging to the Argentine Republic to be allotted number 3 by the Argentine National Authority, her sail shall be marked:

FD
A3

When there is insufficient space to place the letter or letters showing the yacht's nationality in front of her allotted number, it shall be placed above the number.

(d) (i) The class emblems, letters or number, national letters and distinguishing numbers shall be grouped so that the center of the group is above half height; shall sharply contrast in color with the sail; and shall be placed at different heights on the two sides of the sail, those on the starboard side being uppermost, to avoid confusion owing to translucency of the sail.
(ii) Where the class emblem, letter or number is of such a design that when placed back to back on the two sides of the sail they coincide, they may be so placed.
(iii) When **racing** in foreign waters, the national letters and distinguishing numbers only shall be similarly placed on both sides of the spinnaker, but at approximately half height.
(iv) When **racing** in home waters, the distinguishing numbers only need be placed in accordance with rule 25.1(d) (iii).
(e) The following minimum sizes for national letters and distinguishing numbers are prescribed:—
Height: one-tenth of the measurement of the foot of the mainsail rounded up to the nearest 50 mm.
Width: (excluding figure 1 and letter I) 70% of the height.
Thickness: 15% of the height.
Space between adjoining letters and numbers: 20% of the height.

Classes which have a variable sail plan shall specify in their class rules the sizes of letters and numbers, which shall, if practicable, conform to the above requirements.

2(*a*) Unless otherwise authorized by the Race Committee or provided by class rules, a yacht not in one of the classes above shall carry her class number, letter or emblem and her racing number on her mainsail and spinnaker, as provided above, except that the only size requirement may be as an alternative that the numbers, letters and emblems shall be not less than 10 inches in height for yachts under 22 feet waterline length, not less than 15 inches in height for yachts 22 feet to 32 feet waterline and not less than 18 inches in height for yachts over 32 feet waterline length.

(*b*) Offshore racing yachts shall carry N.A.Y.R.U. numbers on mainsails, spinnakers and all overlapping headsails whose LP measurement exceeds 130%.

3. A yacht shall not be disqualified for infringing the provisions of rule 25 without prior warning and adequate opportunity to make correction.

26—Advertisements

1. The hull, crew or equipment of a yacht shall not display any form of advertisement except that:—

(*a*) One sailmaker's mark (which may include the name or mark of the manufacturer of the sail cloth) may be displayed on each side of any sail. The whole of such mark shall be placed not more than 15% of the length of the foot of the sail or 300 mm from its tack whichever is the greater. This latter limitation shall not apply to the position of marks on spinnakers.

(*b*) One builder's mark (which may include the name or mark of the designer) may be placed on the hull, and one maker's mark may be displayed on spars and equipment.

2. Marks (or plates) shall fit within a square not exceeding 150 mm × 150 mm (6 × 6 ins).

3. A yacht shall not be disqualified for infringing the provisions of this rule without prior warning and adequate opportunity to make correction.

27—Forestays and Jib Tacks

Unless otherwise prescribed in the class rules, forestays and jib tacks (excluding spinnaker staysails when not **close-hauled**) shall be fixed approximately in the center-line of the yacht.

28—Flags

A yacht may display her private signal on the leech of her mainsail or from her mizzen mast head, and a wind indicator of a solid color or a feather. Other flags shall not be displayed except for signaling. A yacht shall not be disqualified for failing to comply with the provisions of this rule without warning and adequate opportunity to make correction.

(Numbers 29 and 30 are spare numbers.)

Part IV—Sailing Rules When Yachts Meet

Helmsman's Rights and Obligations Concerning Right of Way: *The rules of Part IV apply only between yachts which either are intending to* **race** *or are* **racing** *in the same or different races, and, except when rule 3.2 (b) (ii) applies, replace the International Regulations for Preventing Collisions at Sea or Government Right-of-Way Rules applicable to the area concerned, from the time a yacht intending to* **race** *begins to sail about in the vicinity of the starting line until she has either* **finished** *or retired and has left the vicinity of the course.*

SECTION A—RULES WHICH ALWAYS APPLY

31—Disqualification

1. A yacht may be disqualified or otherwise penalized for infringing a rule of Part IV only when the infringement occurs while she is **racing**, whether or not a collision results.

2. A yacht may be disqualified before or after she is **racing** for seriously hindering a yacht which is **racing**, or for infringing the sailing instructions.

32—Avoiding Collisions

A right-of-way yacht which fails to make a reasonable attempt to avoid a collision resulting in serious damage may be disqualified as well as the other yacht.

33—Retiring from Race

A yacht which realizes she has infringed a racing rule or a sailing instruction is under an obligation to retire promptly; but, when she persists in **racing**, other yachts shall continue to accord her such rights as she may have under the rules of Part IV.

34—Right-of-Way Yacht Altering Course

When one yacht is required to keep clear of another, the right-of-way yacht shall not so alter course as to prevent the other yacht from keeping clear; so as to increase any alteration of course required of the other yacht in order to keep clear; or so as to obstruct her while she is keeping clear, except:
(*a*) to the extent permitted by rule 38.1, Right-of-Way Yacht Luffing after Starting, and
(*b*) when assuming a **proper course** to **start**, unless subject to the second part of rule 44.1(*b*), Yachts Returning to Start.

35—Hailing

1. Except when **luffing** under rule 38.1, Luffing after Starting, a right-of-way yacht which does not hail before or when making an alteration of course which may not be

foreseen by the other yacht may be disqualified as well as the yacht required to keep clear when a collision resulting in serious damage occurs.

2. A yacht which hails when claiming the establishment or termination of an **overlap** or insufficiency of room at a **mark** or **obstruction** thereby helps to support her claim for the purposes of rule 42, Rounding or Passing Marks and Obstructions.

SECTION B—OPPOSITE TACK RULE

36—Fundamental Rule

A **port-tack** yacht shall keep clear of a **starboard-tack** yacht.

SECTION C—SAME TACK RULES

37—Fundamental Rules

1. A **windward yacht** shall keep clear of a **leeward yacht**.
2. A yacht **clear astern** shall keep clear of a yacht **clear ahead**.
3. A yacht which establishes an **overlap** to **leeward** from **clear astern** shall allow the **windward yacht** ample room and opportunity to keep clear, and during the existence of that **overlap** the **leeward yacht** shall not sail above her **proper course**.

38—Right-of-Way Yacht Luffing after Starting

1. **Luffing Rights and Limitations**. After she has **started** and cleared the starting line, a yacht **clear ahead** or a **leeward yacht** may **luff** as she pleases, except that:—
A **leeward yacht** shall not sail above her **proper course** while an **overlap** exists·if, at any time during its existence, the helmsman of the **windward yacht** (when sighting abeam from his normal **station** and sailing no higher

than the **leeward yacht**) has been abreast or forward of the mainmast of the **leeward yacht**.

2. **Overlap Limitations.** For the purpose of this rule: An **overlap** does not exist unless the yachts are clearly within two overall lengths of the longer yacht; and an **overlap** which exists between two yachts when the leading yacht **starts**, or when one or both of them completes a **tack** or **jibe**, shall be regarded as a new **overlap** beginning at that time.

3. **Hailing to Stop or Prevent a Luff.** When there is doubt, the **leeward yacht** may assume that she has the right to **luff** unless the helmsman of the **windward yacht** has hailed "Mast Abeam", or words to that effect. The **leeward yacht** shall be governed by such hail, and, if she deems it improper, her only remedy is to protest.

4. **Curtailing a Luff.** The **windward yacht** shall not cause a **luff** to be curtailed because of her proximity to the **leeward yacht** unless an **obstruction**, a third yacht or other object restricts her ability to respond.

5. **Luffing Two or More Yachts.** A yacht shall not **luff** unless she has the right to **luff** all yachts which would be affected by her **luff**, in which case they shall all respond even if an intervening yacht or yachts would not otherwise have the right to **luff**.

39—Sailing Below a Proper Course

A yacht which is on a free leg of the course shall not sail below her **proper course** when she is clearly within three of her overall lengths of either a **leeward yacht** or a yacht **clear astern** which is steering a course to pass to **leeward**.

40—Right-of-Way Yacht Luffing before Starting

Before a yacht has **started** and cleared the starting line, any **luff** on her part which causes another yacht to have to alter course to avoid a collision shall be carried out slowly and in such a way so as to give the **windward yacht** room and opportunity to keep clear, but the **leeward yacht** shall not so **luff** above a **close-hauled** course, unless the helmsman of the **windward yacht** (sighting abeam from his normal station) is abaft the mainmast of the **leeward yacht**. Rules 38.3, Hailing to Stop or Prevent a Luff; 38.4, Curtailing a Luff; and 38.5, Luffing Two or more Yachts, also apply.

SECTION D—CHANGING TACK RULES

41—Tacking or Jibing

1. A yacht which is either **tacking** or **jibing** shall keep clear of a yacht **on a tack**.

2. A yacht shall neither **tack** nor **jibe** into a position which will give her right of way unless she does so far enough from a yacht **on a tack** to enable this yacht to keep clear without having to begin to alter her course until after the **tack** or **jibe** has been completed.

3. A yacht which **tacks** or **jibes** has the onus of satisfying the Race Committee that she completed her **tack** or **jibe** in accordance with rule 41.2.

4. When two yachts are both **tacking** or both **jibing** at the same time, the one on the other's **port** side shall keep clear.

SECTION E—RULES OF EXCEPTION AND SPECIAL APPLICATION

When a rule of this section applies, to the extent to which it explicitly provides rights and obligations, it overrides any conflicting rule of Part IV which precedes it except the rules of Section A—Rules Which Always Apply.

42—Rounding or Passing Marks and Obstructions

1. **Fundamental Rules Regarding Room.** When yachts either on the same **tack** or, after **starting** and clearing the starting line, on opposite **tacks**, are about to round or pass

a **mark** on the same required side, with the exception of a starting **mark** surrounded by navigable water, or an **obstruction** on the same side:—

(*a*) When **Overlapped:**

(i) An outside yacht shall give each yacht **overlapping** her on the inside, room to round or pass the **mark** or **obstruction**, except as provided in rules 42.1(*a*) (iii), and (iv) and 42.3. Room includes room for an **overlapping** yacht to **tack** or **jibe** when either is an integral part of the rounding or passing maneuver.

(ii) When an inside yacht of two or more **overlapped** yachts either on opposite **tacks**, or on the same **tack** without **luffing** rights, will have to **jibe** in order most directly to assume a **proper course** to the next **mark**, she shall **jibe** at the first reasonable opportunity.

(iii) When two yachts on opposite **tacks** are on a **beat** or when one of them will have to **tack** either to round the **mark** or to avoid the **obstruction**, as between each other, rule 42.1(*a*)(i) shall not apply and they are subject to rules 36, Opposite Tack Fundamental Rule, and 41, Tacking or Jibing.

(iv) An outside **leeward yacht** with luffing rights may take an inside yacht to windward of a **mark** provided that she hails to that effect and begins to **luff** before she is within two of her overall lengths of the **mark** and provided that she also passes to windward of it.

(*b*) When **Clear Astern** and **Clear Ahead:**

(i) A yacht **clear astern** shall keep clear in anticipation of and during the rounding or passing maneuver when the yacht **clear ahead** remains on the same **tack** or **jibes**.

(ii) A yacht **clear ahead** which **tacks** to round a **mark** is subject to rule 41, Tacking or Jibing, but a yacht **clear astern** shall not **luff** above **close-hauled** so as to prevent the yacht **clear ahead** from **tacking**.

2. **Restrictions on Establishing and Maintaining an Overlap.**

(*a*) A yacht **clear astern** shall not establish an inside **overlap** and be entitled to room under rule 42.1(*a*) (i) when the yacht **clear ahead:**—

(i) is within two of her over-all lengths of the **mark** or **obstruction**, except as provided in rules 42.2(*b*) and

42.2(*c*), or

(ii) is unable to give the required room.

(*b*) The two-lengths determinative above shall not apply to yachts, of which one has completed a **tack** within two overall lengths of a **mark** or an **obstruction**.

(*c*) A yacht **clear astern** may establish an **overlap** between the yacht **clear ahead** and a continuing **obstruction** such as a shoal or the shore, only when there is room for her to do so in safety.

(*d*) (i) A yacht **clear ahead** shall be under no obligation to give room to a yacht **clear astern** before an **overlap** is established.

(ii) A yacht which claims an inside **overlap** has the onus of satisfying the Race Committee that the **overlap** was established in proper time.

(*e*) (i) When an outside yacht is **overlapped** at the time she comes within two of her overall lengths of a **mark**, or an **obstruction**, she shall continue to be bound by rule 42.1(*a*) (i) to give room as required even though the **overlap** may thereafter be broken.

(ii) An outside yacht which claims to have broken an **overlap** has the onus of satisfying the Race Committee that she became **clear ahead** when she was more than two of her overall lengths from the **mark** or an **obstruction**.

3. **At a Starting Mark Surrounded by Navigable Water** When approaching the starting line to **start**, a **leeward yacht** shall be under no obligation to give any **windward yacht** room to pass to leeward of a starting **mark** surrounded by navigable water; but, after the starting signal, a **leeward yacht** shall not deprive a **windward yacht** of room at such a **mark** by sailing either above the course to the first **mark** or above **close-hauled**.

43—Close-Hauled, Hailing for Room to Tack at Obstructions

1. **Hailing**. When two **close-hauled** yachts are on the same **tack** and safe pilotage requires the yacht **clear ahead** or the **leeward yacht** to make a substantial alteration of course to clear an **obstruction**, and if she intends to **tack**,

but cannot **tack** without colliding with the other yacht, she shall hail the other yacht for room to **tack** and clear the other yacht, but she shall not hail and **tack** simultaneously.

2. .**Responding**. The hailed yacht at the earliest possible moment after the hail shall either:—

(*a*) **tack**, in which case, the hailing yacht shall begin to **tack** either:—

(i) before the hailed yacht has completed her **tack**,

(ii) if she cannot then **tack** without colliding with the hailed yacht, immediately she is able to **tack** and clear her, or

(*b*) reply "You **tack**", or words to that effect, if in her opinion she can keep clear without **tacking** or after postponing her **tack**. In this case:—

(i) the hailing yacht shall immediately **tack** and

(ii) the hailed yacht shall keep clear.

(iii) The onus shall lie on the hailed yacht which replied "You **tack**" to satisfy the Race Committee that she kept clear.

3. **Limitation on Right to Room when the Obstruction is a Mark.**

(*a*) When the hailed yacht can fetch an **obstruction** which is also a **mark**, the hailing yacht shall not be entitled to room to **tack** and clear the other yacht and the hailed yacht shall immediately so inform the hailing yacht.

(*b*) If, thereafter, the hailing yacht again hails for room to **tack** and clear the other yacht she shall, after receiving it, retire immediately.

(*c*) If, after having refused to respond to a hail under rule 43.3(*a*), the hailed yacht fails to fetch, she shall retire immediately.

44—Yachts Returning to Start

1.(*a*) A premature starter when returning to **start**, or a yacht working into position from the course side of the starting line or its extensions, when the starting signal is made, shall keep clear of all yachts which are **starting**, or have **started**, correctly, until she is wholly on the pre-start side of the starting line or its extensions.

(*b*) Thereafter, she shall be accorded the rights under the rules of Part IV of a yacht which is **starting** correctly; but if she thereby acquires right of way over another yacht which is **starting** correctly, she shall allow that yacht ample room and opportunity to keep clear.

2. A premature starter while continuing to sail the course and until it is obvious that she is returning to **start**, shall be accorded the rights under the rules of Part IV of a yacht which has **started**.

45—Yachts Re-rounding after Touching a Mark

1. A yacht which has touched a **mark** and is about to exonerate herself in accordance with rule 52.2, Touching a Mark, shall keep clear of all other yachts which are about to round or pass it or have rounded or passed it correctly, until she has rounded it completely and has cleared it and is on a **proper course** to the next **mark**.

2. A yacht which has touched a **mark**, while continuing to sail the course and until it is obvious that she is returning to round it completely in accordance with rule 52.2, Touching a Mark, shall be accorded rights under the rules of Part IV.

SECTION F—WHEN NOT UNDER WAY

46—Anchored, Aground or Capsized

1. A yacht under way shall keep clear of another yacht **racing** which is anchored, aground or capsized. Of two anchored yachts, the one which anchored later shall keep clear, except that a yacht which is dragging shall keep clear of one which is not.

2. A yacht anchored or aground shall indicate the fact to any yacht which may be in danger of fouling her. Unless the size of the yachts or the weather conditions make some other signal necessary a hail is sufficient indication.

3. A yacht shall not be penalized for fouling a yacht in distress which she is attempting to assist or a yacht which goes aground or capsizes immediately ahead of her.

(Numbers 47 and 48 are spare numbers.)

Obligations of Helmsman and Crew in Handling a Yacht: *Except for rule 49, a yacht is subject to the rules of Part V only while she is* **racing.**

49—Fair Sailing

A yacht shall attempt to win a race only by fair sailing, superior speed and skill, and, except in team races, by individual effort. However, a yacht may be disqualified under this rule only in the case of a clear-cut violation of the above principles and only if no other rule applies.

50—Ranking as a Starter

A yacht whose entry has been accepted by the Race Committee and which sails about in the vicinity of the starting line between her preparatory and starting signals shall rank as a starter, even if she does not **start.**

51—Sailing the Course

1.(*a*) A yacht shall **start** and **finish** only as prescribed in the starting and finishing definition.

(*b*) Unless otherwise prescribed in the sailing instructions, a yacht which either crosses prematurely, or is on the course side of the starting line, or its extensions, at the starting signal, shall return and **start** in accordance with the definition.

(*c*) Unless otherwise prescribed in the sailing instructions, when after a general recall, any part of a yacht's hull, crew or equipment is on the course side of the starting line or its extensions during the minute before her starting signal, she shall thereafter return to the pre-start side of the line across one of its extensions and **start.**

(*d*) Failure of a yacht to see or hear her recall notification shall not relieve her of her obligation to **start** correctly.

2. A yacht shall sail the course so as to round or pass

each **mark** on the required side in correct sequence, and so that a string representing her wake from the time she **starts** until she **finishes** would, when drawn taut, lie on the required side of each **mark**.

3. A **mark** has a required side for a yacht as long as she is on a leg which it begins, bounds or ends. A starting line **mark** begins to have a required side for a yacht when she **starts**. A starting limit **mark** has a required side for a yacht from the time she is approaching the starting line to **start** until she has left it astern on the first leg. A finishing line **mark** and a finishing limit **mark** cease to have a required side for a yacht as soon as she **finishes**.

4. A yacht which rounds or passes a **mark** on the wrong side may exonerate herself by making her course conform to the requirements of rule 51.2.

5. It is not necessary for a yacht to cross the finishing line completely; after **finishing** she may clear it in either direction.

6. In the absence of the Race Committee, a yacht shall take her own time when she finishes, and report the time taken to the Race Committee as soon as possible. If there is no longer an established finishing line, the finishing line shall be a line extending from the required side of the finishing **mark** at right angles to the last leg of the course, and 100 yards long or as much longer as may be necessary to insure adequate depth of water in crossing it.

52—Touching a Mark

1. A yacht which either:—
(a) touches:—
   (i) a starting **mark** before **starting**;
   (ii) a **mark** which begins, bounds or ends the leg of the course on which she is sailing; or
   (iii) a finishing **mark** after **finishing**, or
(b) causes a **mark** or **mark** vessel to shift to avoid being touched,
shall immediately retire, unless either:
   (i) she alleges that she was wrongfully compelled by another yacht to touch it or cause it to shift, in which case she shall protest; or

(ii) she exonerates herself in accordance with rule 52.2.
2.(*a*) Unless otherwise prescribed in the sailing instructions, a yacht which touches a **mark** surrounded by navigable water may exonerate herself by completing one entire rounding of the **mark**, leaving it on the required side, and thereafter she shall re-round or re-pass it, without touching it, as required to sail the course in accordance with rule 51, Sailing the Course, and the sailing instructions.

(*b*) When a yacht touches:

(i) a starting **mark**, she shall carry out the rounding after she has **started**; or

(ii) a finishing **mark**, she shall carry out the rounding, and she shall not rank as having **finished** until she has completed the rounding and again crosses the finishing line in accordance with the definition of **finishing**.

53—Fog Signals and Lights

1. Every yacht shall observe the International Regulations for Preventing Collisions at Sea or Government Rules and fog signals and, as a minimum, the carrying of lights at night.

2. The use of additional special purpose lights such as masthead, spreader or jib luff lights shall not constitute grounds for protest.

54—Setting and Sheeting Sails

1. **Changing Sails**. While changing headsails and spinnakers a replacing sail may be fully set and trimmed before the sail it replaces is taken in, but only one mainsail and, except when changing, only one spinnaker shall be carried set.

2. **Sheeting Sails to Spars**. Unless otherwise prescribed by the class rules, any sail may be sheeted to or led above a boom regularly used for a working sail and permanently attached to the mast to which the head of the working sail is set, but no sails shall be sheeted over or through outriggers. An outrigger is any fitting so placed, except as permitted in the first sentence of rule 54.2, that it could exert outward pressure on a sheet at a point from which, with

the yacht upright, a vertical line would fall outside the hull or deck planking at that point, or outside such other position as class rules prescribe. For the purpose of this rule: bulwarks, rails and rubbing strakes are not part of the hull or deck planking. A boom of a boomed headsail which requires no adjustment when **tacking** is not an outrigger.

3. **Spinnaker, Spinnaker Pole**. A spinnaker shall not be set without a pole. The tack of a spinnaker when set and drawing shall be in close proximity to the outboard end of a spinnaker pole. Any headsail may be attached to a spinnaker pole provided a spinnaker is not set. A sail tacked down abaft the foremost mast is not a headsail. Only one spinnaker pole shall be used at a time and when in use shall be carried only on the side of the foremost mast opposite to the main boom and shall be fixed to the mast. Rule 54.3 shall not apply when shifting a spinnaker pole or sail attached thereto.

55—Owner Steering Another Yacht

An owner shall not steer any yacht other than his own in a race wherein his own yacht competes, without the previous consent of the Race Committee.

56—Boarding

Unless otherwise prescribed in the sailing instructions, no person shall board a yacht except for the purpose of rule 58, Rendering Assistance, or to attend an injured or ill member of the crew or temporarily as one of the crew of a vessel fouled.

57—Leaving, Man Overboard

Unless otherwise prescribed in the sailing instructions, no person on board a yacht when her preparatory signal was made shall leave, unless injured or ill, or for the purposes of rule 58, Rendering Assistance, except that any member of the crew may fall overboard or leave her to swim, stand on the bottom as a means of anchoring, haul her out ashore to effect repairs, reef sails or bail out, or help her to get clear after grounding or fouling another vessel or object, provided that this person is back on board before the yacht continues in the race.

58—Rendering Assistance

Every yacht shall render all possible assistance to any vessel or person in peril, when in a position to do so.

59—Outside Assistance

Except as permitted by rules 56, Boarding, 58, Rendering Assistance, and 64, Aground or Foul of an Obstruction, a yacht shall neither receive outside assistance nor use any gear other than that on board when her preparatory signal was made.

60—Means of Propulsion

A yacht shall be propelled only by the natural action of the wind on the sails, spars and hull, and water on the hull, and shall not pump, "ooch" or rock, as described in Appendix 2, nor check way by abnormal means, except for the purpose of rule 58, Rendering Assistance, or of recovering a man who has accidentally fallen overboard. An oar, paddle or other object may be used in emergency for steering. An anchor may be sent out in a boat only as permitted by rule 64, Aground or Foul of an Obstruction.

61—Sounding

Any means of sounding may be used provided rule 60, Means of Propulsion, is not infringed.

62—Manual Power

A yacht shall use manual power only, except that a power winch or windlass may be used in weighing anchor or in getting clear after running aground or fouling any object, and a power bilge pump may be used in an auxiliary yacht.

63—Anchoring and Making Fast

1. A yacht may anchor. Means of anchoring may include the crew standing on the bottom and any weight lowered to the bottom. A yacht shall recover any anchor or weight used, and any chain or rope attached to it, before continuing in the race, unless after making every effort she finds recovery impossible. In this case she shall report the circumstances to the Race Committee, which may disqualify her if it considers the loss due either to inadequate gear or to insufficient effort to recover it.

2. A yacht shall be afloat and off moorings, before her preparatory signal, but may be anchored, and shall not thereafter make fast or be made fast by means other than anchoring, nor be hauled out, except for the purpose of rule 64, Aground or Foul of an Obstruction, or to effect repairs, reef sails or bail out.

64—Aground or Foul of an Obstruction

A yacht, after grounding or fouling another vessel or other object, is subject to rule 62, Manual Power, and may, in getting clear, use her own anchors, boats, ropes, spars and other gear; may send out an anchor in a boat; may be refloated by her crew going overboard either to stand on the bottom or to go ashore to push off; but may receive outside assistance only from the crew of the vessel fouled. A yacht shall recover all her own gear used in getting clear before continuing in the race.

65—Skin Friction

A yacht shall not eject or release from a container any substance (such as polymer) the purpose of which is, or could be, to reduce the frictional resistance of the hull by altering the character of the flow of water inside the boundary layer.

66—Increasing Stability

Unless otherwise prescribed by her class rules or in the sailing instructions, a yacht shall not use any device, such as a trapeze or plank, to project outboard the weight of any of the crew, nor, when a yacht is equipped with lifelines, shall any member of the crew station any part of his torso outside them, other than temporarily.

Part VI—Protests, Disqualifications and Appeals

67—Contact between Yachts Racing

1. When there is contact between the hull, spars, standing rigging or crew of two yachts while racing, both shall be disqualified, unless one of them retires in acknowledgement of an infringement of the rules, or one or both of them acts in accordance with rule 68.3, Protests.

2. A third yacht which witnesses an apparent collision between two yachts and, after finishing or retiring, discovers that neither of them has observed rule 67.1, is relieved by rule 68.3(*b*) from the requirement of showing a protest flag and may lodge a protest against them.

3. The Race Committee may waive this rule when it is satisfied that minor contact was unavoidable.

68—Protests

1. A yacht can protest against any other yacht, except that a protest for an alleged infringement of the rules of Part IV can be made only by a yacht directly involved in, or witnessing an incident.

2. A protest occurring between yachts competing in

separate races sponsored by different clubs shall be heard
by a combined committee of both clubs.

3.(*a*) A protest for an infringement of the rules or sailing
instructions occurring during a race shall be signified by
showing a flag (International Code flag "B" is always
acceptable, irrespective of any other provisions in the sailing instructions) conspicuously in the rigging of the protesting yacht at the first reasonable opportunity and
keeping it flying until she has **finished** or retired, or if
the first reasonable opportunity occurs after **finishing**,
until acknowledged by the Race Committee. In the case
of a yacht sailed singlehanded, it will be sufficient if the
flag (whether displayed in the rigging or not) is brought
to the notice of the yacht protested against as soon as
possible after the incident and to the Race Committee
when the protesting yacht **finishes**.

(*b*) A yacht which has no knowledge of the facts justifying
a protest until after she has **finished** or retired may
nevertheless protest without having shown a protest flag.

(*c*) A protesting yacht shall try to inform the yacht protested against that a protest will be lodged.

(*d*) Such a protest shall be in writing and be signed by
the owner or his representative, and include the following particulars:

(i) The date, time and whereabouts of the incident.

(ii) The particular rule or rules or sailing instructions
alleged to have been infringed.

(iii) A statement of the facts.

(iv) Unless irrelevant, a diagram of the incident.

(*e*) Unless otherwise prescribed in the sailing instructions
a protesting yacht shall deliver, or if that is not possible,
mail her protest to the Race Committee:

(i) within two hours of the time she **finishes** the race,
or within such time as may have been prescribed in
the sailing instructions under rule 3.2(*b*) (xv), unless
the Race Committee has reason to extend these time
limits, or

(ii) when she does not **finish** the race, within such a
time as the Race Committee may consider reasonable
in the circumstances of the case.

A protest shall be accompanied by such fee, if any, as
may have been prescribed in the sailing instructions

under rule 3.2(*b*) (xv).

(*f*) The Race Committee shall allow the protestor to remedy at a later time:

(i) any defects in the details required by rule 68.3(*d*) provided that the protest includes a summary of the facts, and

(ii) a failure to deposit such fee as may be required under rule 68.3(*e*) and prescribed in the sailing instructions.

4.(*a*) A protest that a measurement, scantling or flotation rule has been infringed while **racing**, or that a classification or rating certificate is for any reason invalid, shall be lodged with the Race Committee not later than 1800 hours on the day following the race. The Race Committee shall send a copy of the protest to the yacht protested against and, when there appears to be reasonable grounds for the protest, it shall refer the question to an authority qualified to decide such questions. (See Appendix 6)

(*b*) Deviations in excess of tolerances stated in the class rules caused by normal wear or damage and which do not affect the performance of the yacht shall not invalidate the measurement or rating certificate of the yacht for a particular race, but shall be rectified before she **races** again, unless in the opinion of the Race Committee there has been no practical opportunity to rectify the wear or damage.

(*c*) The Race Committee, in making its decision, shall be governed by the determination of such authority. Copies of such decision shall be sent to all yachts involved.

5.(*a*) A yacht which alleges that her chances of winning a prize have been prejudiced by an action or omission of the Race Committee, may seek redress from the Race Committee in accordance with the requirements for a protest provided in rules 68.3(*d*), (*e*) and (*f*). In these circumstances a protest flag need not be shown.

(*b*) When the Race Committee decides that such action or omission was prejudicial, and that the result of the race was altered thereby, it shall cancel or **abandon** the race, or make such other arrangement as it deems equitable.

6. A protest made in writing shall not be withdrawn, but

shall be decided by the Race Committee, unless prior to the hearing full responsibility is acknowledged by one or more yachts.

7. Alternative Penalties. When so prescribed in the sailing instructions, the procedure and penalty for infringing a rule of Part IV shall be as provided in Appendix 3, Alternative Penalties for Infringement of a Rule of Part IV.

69—Refusal of a Protest

1. When the Race Committee decides that a protest does not conform to the requirements of rule 68, Protests, it shall inform the protesting yacht that her protest will not be heard and of the reasons for such decision.

2. Such a decision shall not be reached without giving the protesting yacht all opportunity of bringing evidence that the requirements of rule 68, Protests, were complied with.

70—Hearings

1. When the Race Committee decides that a protest conforms to all the requirements of rule 68, Protests, it shall call a hearing as soon as possible. The protest, or a copy of it, shall be made available to all yachts involved, and each shall be notified, in writing if practicable, of the time and place set for the hearing. A reasonable time shall be allowed for the preparation of defense. At the hearing, the Race Committee shall take the evidence presented by the parties to the protest and such other evidence as it may consider necessary. The parties to the protest, or a representative of each, shall have the right to be present, but all others, except one witness at a time while testifying, may be excluded. A yacht other than one named in the protest, which is involved in that protest, shall have all the rights of yachts originally named in it.

2. A yacht shall not be penalized without a hearing, except as provided in rule 73.1(*a*), Disqualification without Protest.

3. Failure on the part of any of the interested parties or a representative to make an effort to attend the hearing of

the protest may justify the Race Committee in deciding the protest as it thinks fit without a full hearing.

71—Decisions

The Race Committee shall make its decision promptly after the hearing. Each decision shall be communicated to the parties involved, and shall state fully the facts and grounds on which it is based and shall specify the rules, if any, infringed. If requested by any of the parties, such decision shall be given in writing and shall include the Race Committee's diagram. The findings of the Race Committee as to the facts involved shall be final.

72—Disqualification after Protest

1. When the Race Committee, after hearing a protest or acting under rule 73, Disqualification without Protest, or any appeal authority, is satisfied:—
   (a) that a yacht has infringed any of these rules or the sailing instructions, or
   (b) that in consequence of her neglect of any of these rules or the sailing instructions she has compelled other yachts to infringe any of these rules or the sailing instructions,
she shall be disqualified unless the sailing instructions applicable to that race provide some other penalty. Such disqualification or other penalty shall be imposed, irrespective of whether the rule or sailing instruction which led to the disqualification or penalty was mentioned in the protest, or the yacht which was at fault was mentioned or protested against, e.g., the protesting yacht or a third yacht might be disqualified and the protested yacht absolved.

2. For the purpose of awarding points in a series, a retirement after an infringement of any of these rules or the sailing instructions shall not rank as a disqualification. This penalty can be imposed only in accordance with rules 72, Disqualification after Protest, and 73, Disqualification without Protest.

3. When a yacht either is disqualified or has retired, the next in order shall be awarded her place.

73—Disqualification without Protest

1.(*a*) A yacht which fails either to **start** or to **finish** may be disqualified without protest or hearing, after the conclusion of the race, except that she shall be entitled to a hearing, provided she satisfies the Race Committee that an error may have been made.

(*b*) A yacht so penalized shall be informed of the action taken, either by letter or by notification in the racing results.

2. When the Race Committee:—

(*a*) sees an apparent infringement by a yacht of any of these rules or the sailing instructions (except as provided in rule 73.1), or

(*b*) has reasonable grounds for believing that an infringement resulted in serious damage, or

(*c*) receives a report not later than the same day from a witness who was neither competing in the race, nor otherwise an interested party, alleging an infringement, or

(*d*) has reasonable grounds for supposing from the evidence at the hearing of a valid protest, that any yacht involved in the incident may have committed such an infringement,

it may notify such yacht thereof orally, or if that is not possible, in writing, delivered or mailed not later than 1800 hours on the day after:—

(i) the finish of the race, or

(ii) the receipt of the report, or

(iii) the hearing of the protest.

Such notice shall contain a statement of the pertinent facts and of the particular rule or rules or sailing instructions believed to have been infringed, and the Race Committee shall act thereon in the same manner as if it had been a protest made by a competitor.

74—Penalties for Gross Infringement of Rules

1. When a gross infringement of any of these rules, the sailing instructions or class rules is proved against the owner, the owner's representative, the helmsman or sailing

master of a yacht, such persons may be disqualified by the National Authority, for any period it may think fit, from either steering or sailing in a yacht in any race held under its jurisdiction.

2. Notice of any penalty adjudged under this rule shall be communicated to the I.Y.R.U. which shall inform all National Authorities.

3. After a gross breach of good manners or sportsmanship the Race Committee may exclude a competitor from further participation in a series or take other disciplinary action.

75—Persons Interested not to take part in Decision

1. No member of either a Race Committee or of any appeals authority shall take part in the discussion or decision upon any disputed question in which he is an interested party, but this does not preclude him from giving evidence in such a case.

2. The term "interested party" includes anyone who stands to gain or lose as a result of the decision.

76—Expenses Incurred by Protest

Unless otherwise prescribed by the Race Committee, the fees and expenses entailed by a protest on measurement or classification shall be paid by the unsuccessful party.

77—Appeals

1. **Limitations on Right to Appeal**—Appeals involving solely the interpretation of the racing rules may be taken to the Appeals Committee of the Union for final determination:

(a) If the Club is a member of the Union but is not a member of a local association or district belonging to the Union, by an owner or his representative from a decision of the Race Committee;

(b) If the Club is a member of a local association or dis-

trict belonging to the Union by an owner or his representative or by the Race Committee from a decision of the
local association or district.

2. **Appeal Procedure**—(*a*) A notice of appeal shall be
mailed, not later than ten days from receipt of the written
decision, to the body rendering the decision, preferably
with a copy to the Appeals Committee, and shall contain
the grounds for the appeal, that is to say, how the appellant
believes the rules should be interpreted and his reasons
therefor.

(*b*) The body rendering the decision shall promptly notify
the other parties involved, sending them a copy of the
notice of appeal.

(*c*) In an appeal to the Union the body rendering the
decision shall promptly file, in writing, with the Secretary
of the Union all particulars called for by rule 78, Particulars to be Provided in Appeals.

3. **Decision of Appeals Committee**—Decisions of the
Appeals Committee shall be in writing and the grounds of
each decision shall be specified therein. Each decision shall
be filed with the Secretary of the Union, who shall send
copies thereof to all parties to the infringement and appeal.

78—Particulars to be Supplied in Appeals

An appeal to the Union shall include the following particulars so far as they are applicable:

1. A copy of the protest or protests, request for relief or
statement by the Race Committee acting under rule 73.2,
as the case may be, together with all other written statements which may have been put in by the parties.

2. The names or numbers of the yachts represented at
the hearing, and of any yacht duly notified of the hearing,
but not represented, and the name and address of the representative of each of said yachts.

3. A copy of the sailing instructions.

4. A copy of the decision of the Race Committee contain-
ing a full statement of the facts found by it, its decision and
the grounds therefor.

5. An official diagram prepared by the Race Committee
in accordance with the facts found by it and signed by it

and showing (i) the course to the next **mark** or, if close by, the **mark** itself and its required side, (ii) the direction and velocity of the wind, (iii) the set of the current, if any, and (iv) the position or positions and tracks of the yachts involved.

6. A copy of the decision, if any, of the local association or district.

7. A copy of the notice of appeal, including the grounds thereof.

8. Observations, if any, upon the appeal by any of the parties.

79—Questions of Interpretation

The Appeals Committee will accept and act upon questions involving solely the interpretation of the racing rules but only when submitted by a club or local association or district, from whose decision an appeal may be taken as provided in rule 77.1, Limitations on Right to Appeal. Decisions of such questions may, at the discretion of the Chairman of the Appeals Committee, be acted upon by less than the full committee. Questions should include all the assumed facts, an assumed sailing instruction if pertinent, and a diagram if one will help to clarify the facts. Questions are not acceptable on protest decisions which may be appealed.

TEAM RACING RULES

Team racing shall be sailed under the yacht racing rules of the International Yacht Racing Union as adopted by the North American Yacht Racing Union supplemented as follows:

SAILING RULES

1. A yacht may maneuver against a yacht sailing on another leg of the course only if she can do so while sailing a **proper course** relative to the leg on which she herself is

sailing. For the purpose of this rule, each time a leg is sailed it shall be regarded as "another leg of the course."

2. Except to protect her own or a team mate's finishing position, a yacht in one team which is completing the last leg of the course shall not maneuver against a yacht in another team which has no opponent astern of her.

3. Right of way may be waived by team mates, provided that in so doing, I.Y.R.U. rule 34, Right-of-Way Yacht Altering Course, is not infringed in respect to an opponent; but if contact occurs between them and neither retires immediately, the poorer finishing team mate shall automatically be disqualified.

The benefits of rule 12, Yacht Materially Prejudiced, shall not be available to a yacht damaged by contact between team mates.

4. When two **overlapping** yachts on the same **tack** are in the act of rounding or passing on the required side of a **mark** at which their **proper course** changes:

(*a*) If the **leeward yacht** is inside, she may, if she has **luffing** rights hold her course or **luff**. If she does not have **luffing** rights, she shall promptly assume her **proper course** to the next **mark** whether or not she has to **jibe**;

(*b*) If the **windward yacht** is inside, she shall promptly **luff** up to her **proper course** to the next **mark**, or if she cannot assume such **proper course** without **tacking** and does not choose to **tack**, she shall promptly **luff** up to **close-hauled**. This clause does not restrict **a leeward yacht's** right to **luff** under rule 38, Luffing after Starting.

SCORING

5. **Each Race**

(*a*) Yachts shall score three-quarters of a point for first place, two points for second place, three points for third place, and so on.

(*b*) A yacht which does not **start** shall score points equal to the number of yachts entitled to **start** in the race.

(*c*) A yacht which infringes any rule and retires with reasonable promptness shall score one point more than the number of yachts entitled to **start** in the race, but if her retirement is tardy, or if she fails to retire and is subsequently disqualified, she shall score four points more than the number of yachts entitled to **start** in the race.

(*d*) A yacht which infringes a rule shortly before or when **finishing** shall be considered to have retired with reasonable promptness if she notifies the Race Committee of her retirement as soon as is reasonably practicable.

(*e*) A yacht which does not **finish** for a reason other than an infringement shall score points equal to the number of yachts entitled to **start** in the race, except as provided in (*f*).

(*f*) After all the yachts of one team have **finished** or retired, the Race Committee may stop the race and award to each yacht of the other team which is still **racing** and under way, the points she would have received had she **finished**.

(*g*) The team with the lowest total point score shall be the winner of the race.

6. Reports and Declarations

(*a*) A yacht which retires shall promptly report that fact and the reason therefor to the Race Committee, and if it resulted from a rule infringement she shall state:

(i) when the infringement occurred;

(ii) which yacht(s), if any, was involved in the infringement; and

(iii) when she retired.

The sailing instructions may require her to submit within a prescribed time a signed statement covering (i), (ii) and (iii).

(*b*) The sailing instructions may require a yacht to sign a declaration within a prescribed time in accordance with rule 14, Award of Prizes, Places and Points.

(*c*) A yacht which fails either:

(i) to report her retirement in accordance with rule 6(*a*) above; or

(ii) to sign such declaration as may be required under rule 6(*b*) above, shall be awarded points on the assumption that she retired tardily owing to a rule infringement.

7. **The Match and Breaking Ties**

(a) When two teams only are competing:

(i) the team winning the greater number of races shall be the winner of the match.

(ii) When there is a tie because each team has won the same number of races it shall be resolved in favor of the winner of the last race.

(b) When more than two teams are competing in a series consisting of races each of which is between two teams:

(i) The team winning the greatest number of races shall be the winner of the match.

(ii) When there is a tie because two or more teams have won the same number of races, the winner shall be the team which has beaten the other tied team or teams in the most races, or if still tied, the team with the lowest point score, or if still tied, the team which beat the other in the last race between them.

(c) When more than two teams are all competing in each race:

(i) The team with the lowest total point score in all races sailed shall be the winner of the match.

(ii) When there is a tie the winner shall be the team which has beaten the other tied team or teams in the most races, or if still tied, the team which beat the other team or teams in the last race.

(d) Notwithstanding the above provisions for breaking ties, a tie shall instead be resolved by a sail-off, if practicable, in which case the time for the sail-off shall be scheduled before the series starts.

Addendum—Rules Recommended to Apply When the Home Team Provides All Racing Yachts

A. Allotment of Yachts. The home team shall provide the visiting team with a list of the yachts to be used and of the sail numbers allotted to each yacht for the match. The home team shall divide these yachts into as many equal groups as there are competing teams and these groups shall be drawn for by lot for the first race. The yachts shall then be allotted to the crews by each team, except that a helmsman shall not at any time steer the yacht of which he is normally the helmsman. The groups of yachts shall be exchanged between races so that, as far as possible, each group will be sailed in turn by each team. In a two-team match after an even number of races, if either team requests that the yachts be regrouped, the home team shall re-divide them into new groups which shall be drawn for by lot; except that for the final odd race of a two-team match, the visiting team may select the group it wishes to sail.

B. **Allotment of Sails**. If sails as well as yachts are provided by the home team, the sails used by each yacht in the first race shall be used by her throughout the series and the substitution of a spare or extra sail shall not be permitted unless because of damage or for some other valid reason, a change is approved by the Race Committee after notification to both teams.

C. **Group Identification**. One group shall carry no markings. The second group shall carry dark colored strips or pennants, and additional groups shall carry light or differently colored strips or pennants. Strips or pennants should usually be provided by the home team and should be attached to the same conspicuous place on each boat of a group, such as the after end of the main boom or permanent backstay.

D. **Breakdowns**. When a breakdown results in substantial loss, the Race Committee shall decide whether or not it was the fault of the crew. In general, a breakdown caused by defective equipment, or the result of a foul by an opponent shall not be deemed the fault of the crew, and a breakdown caused by careless handling or capsizing shall be. In case of doubt, the doubt shall be resolved in favor of the crew.

E. If the Race Committee decides that the breakdown was not the fault of the crew and that a reasonably competent crew could not have remedied the defect in time to prevent substantial loss, it shall cancel the race or order the race to be resailed, or award the breakdown yacht the number of points she would have received had she finished in the same position in the race she held when she broke down. In case of doubt as to her position when she broke down, the doubt shall be resolved against her.

F. **Spares**. The home team shall be prepared to provide one or more extra yachts and sails to replace any which, in the opinion of the Race Committee, are unfit for use in the remaining races.

Appendix I—Amateur

1. For the purpose of international yacht races in which yachts entering are required to have one or more amateurs on board, and in other races with similar requirements, an amateur is a yachtsman who engages in yacht racing as a pastime as distinguished from a means of obtaining a livelihood. No yachtsman shall lose amateur status by reason of the fact that his livelihood is derived from designing or constructing any boats or parts of boats, or accessories of boats, or sails or from other professions associated with the sea and ships.

2. Any yachtsman whose amateur status is questioned or is in doubt, may apply to the National Authority of the country of his residence for recognition of his amateur status. Any such applicant may be required to provide such particulars and evidence and to pay such fee as the National Authority may prescribe. Recognition may be suspended or cancelled by the National Authority by which it was granted.

3. The permanent committee of the International Yacht Racing Union, or any tribunal nominated by the chairman of that committee, may review the decision of any Authority as to the amateur status of a yachtsman for the purpose of competing in international races.

4. For the purposes of participation in the Olympic

Regatta an amateur is required to conform to the eligibility rules of the International Olympic Committee. Information on these eligibility requirements is available from all National Authorities.

Appendix 2—"Pumping" Sails, "Ooching" and "Rocking"

"Pumping" consists of frequent rapid trimming of sails with no particular reference to a change in true or apparent wind direction. To promote planing or surfing, rapid trimming of sails need not be considered "pumping".

The purpose of this interpretation of rule 60 is to prevent "fanning" one's boat around the course by flapping the sail similar to a bird's wing in flight. "Pumping" or **frequent**, quickly-repeated trimming and releasing of the mainsail to increase propulsion is not allowed and is not "the natural action of the wind on the sails".

Similarly, frequent, quickly-repeated jibing or roll-tacking in calm and near calm conditions fall into the same category as "pumping".

Where surfing or planing conditions exist, however, rule 60 allows taking advantage of "the natural action of water on the hull" through the **rapid** trimming of sails and adjustment of helm to **promote** (initiate) surfing or planing.

The test is whether or not the conditions are such that by **rapid** trimming of sails a boat could be **started** surfing or planing. A skipper challenged for "pumping" will have to prove, through the performance either of his own boat or of other boats, that surfing or planing conditions existed, and that the **frequency** of his **rapid** trimming was geared to the **irregular** or **cyclical** wave forms rather than to a **regular** rhythmic pattern.

Note that the interpretation refers to "promoting" and not to "maintaining" surfing or planing. Once a boat has started surfing or planing on a particular set of wave forms, from then on she must let the natural action of wind and water propel her without further **rapid** trimming and releasing of the sails.

Rapid trimming when approaching marks or the finishing line or other critical points should be consistent with that which was practiced throughout the leg.

"Ooching", which consists of lunging forward and stopping abruptly, falls in the same category as "pumping".

"Rocking" consists of persistently rolling a yacht from side to side.

Appendix 3—Alternative Penalties for Infringement of a Rule of Part IV

Experience indicates that the 720° turns penalty is most satisfactory for small boats in relatively short races and it can be dangerous for large boats and not sufficiently severe in long races. The 20% penalty is relatively mild and is designed to encourage acknowledgment of infringements and willingness to protest when not acknowledged. Graduated penalties assign heavier penalties for more serious infringements. All three systems keep yachts racing.

Any one of the three following alternatives to disqualification may be used by including in the sailing instructions a provision such as the following (or if preferred the selected penalty may be quoted in full):—

The 720° turns penalty (or the percentage penalty or graduated penalties) as provided in Appendix 3 of the yacht racing rules will apply instead of disqualification, for infringement of a rule of Part IV.

720° Turns

A yacht which acknowledges infringing a rule of Part IV may exonerate herself by making two full 360° turns (720°) subject to the following provisions:

1. The yacht infringed against shall notify the infringing yacht at the first reasonable opportunity by hail and by showing a protest flag. (The first reasonable opportunity for a hail is usually immediately.)

2. Upon such notification, the yacht acknowledging fault shall immediately start to get well clear of other yachts and while on the same leg of the course she shall hail adjacent yachts of her intention and then make her turns. While so doing, she shall keep clear of all other yachts until she has completed her turns and is on a **proper course** to the next **mark**.

3. For the purpose of applying this penalty, "a leg of the course" shall be deemed terminated when two boat lengths from the **mark** ending that leg, and the next leg shall be deemed to commence at this point except for the final leg

which is terminated when a yacht is no longer **racing**.

4. The turns may be made in either direction but both in the same direction.

5. When the infringement occurs before the starting signal, the infringing yacht shall make her turns after the starting signal and before **starting**.

6. When an infringement occurs at the finishing line, the infringing yacht shall make her turns on the last leg of the course before being officially finished.

7. If neither yacht acknowledges fault, a protest may be lodged in accordance with rule 68, Protests, and the sailing instructions.

8. An infringing yacht shall report her infringement and the resulting action taken by her to the Race Committee, together with such other information as may be required by the sailing instructions.

9. Failure to observe the above requirements will render a yacht which has infringed a rule of Part IV liable to disqualification or other penalty.

10. An infringing yacht involved in a collision which results in serious damage to either yacht shall be liable to disqualification.

Percentage

1. A yacht which acknowledges infringing a rule of Part IV shall be penalized by receiving the score for the place worse than her actual finishing position by 20% to the nearest whole number of the number of starters in that race, except that the penalty shall be at least three places and except further that in no case will she receive a score for a position worse than one more than the number of starters. (Examples: An infringing yacht which finishes eighth in a start of nineteen yachts will receive the score for twelfth place ($19 \times 0.2 = 3.8$ or 4); an infringing yacht which finishes thirteenth in a start of fourteen yachts will receive the score for fifteenth place.)

(*a*) A yacht infringing a rule in more than one incident shall receive a 20% penalty for each incident.

(*b*) The imposition of a 20% penalty on a yacht shall not affect the score of other yachts. (Thus two yachts may receive the same score.)

2. The yacht infringed against shall notify the infringing yacht at the first reasonable opportunity by hail and by showing a protest flag. (The first reasonable opportunity for a hail is usually immediately.)

3. A yacht which acknowledges infringing a rule of Part IV shall at the first reasonable opportunity show International Code flag "I", or such other signal as the sailing instructions may specify, keep it flying until she has finished and report the infringement to the Race Committee.

4. A yacht which fails to acknowledge an infringement as provided in paragraph 3 and which, after a protest and hearing, is found to have infringed a rule of Part IV, shall be penalized 30% or at least five places instead of 20%.

5. A yacht which has shown International Code flag "I" during a race and has not reported the infringement to the Race Committee shall be liable to the 30% penalty of paragraph 4 without a hearing except on the two points of having shown the flag and having reported the infringement to the Race Committee.

6. An infringing yacht involved in a collision which results in serious damage to either yacht shall be liable to disqualification.

Graduated

1. A yacht which infringes a rule of Part IV may continue racing and complete the course, after which she shall have her Finishing Place in that race adjusted by one of the following Penalty Percents; plus the extra 10% of Section 4, when applicable.

2. The following infringements are assigned Specific Penalty Percents, taking precedence over the General Penalty Percents of Section 3:

    a. Infringement of Rule 42.3, the "anti-barging" rule   40%

    b. Infringement of Rule 42.2(a), "forcing an over-lap" at a Mark or Obstruction   40%

    c. Infringement of Rule 36 (port-tack yacht keep clear) if, while heading for the line to start or on any windward leg, the starboard-tack yacht is forced to tack to avoid collision; or because of collision   40%

d. Infringement of Rule 44, Yachts Returning to Start; or infringement when the yachts are on different legs of the course   40%

e. Touching a mark, if a rerounding was not properly performed in accordance with Rule 52.2; or if that section is suspended by the Sailing Instructions   20%

f. If the innocent yacht is recorded as DNS or DNF because of collision damage; or because of collision injury to personnel   100%

3. Other than the Penalty Percents specified above in Section 2 and in Section 4 below, the following General Penalty Percents shall apply for infringements of Part IV. The one fact to be determined is whether or not the innocent yacht lost position to the infringing yacht. Position is deemed lost if the infringing yacht crosses ahead; or if she tacks or jibes too close; or if she terminates the overlap in any way other than by dropping clear astern. No position is deemed lost if an overlapping infringing yacht terminates the overlap by dropping clear astern; or if the infringement occurs before the innocent yacht heads for the line to start.

a. Position lost to the infringing yacht   40%

b. No position lost to the infringing yacht   20%

4. If an infringing yacht acknowledges her fault by a reasonably prompt hail (such as "my fault" or words to that effect) and by showing International Code Flag "I" (or such other signal as the Sailing Instructions may specify), the applicable Penalty Percent of Section 2 or 3 shall be used. If fault is NOT so acknowledged, but is later admitted or decided by a protest hearing, then an extra 10% shall be added. The specified signal shall be kept flying by the infringing yacht until she has finished and reported her infringement to the Race Committee.

5. Infringement of a Rule of NAYRU's Part III (General Requirements) or Part V (Other Sailing Rules) may, at the discretion of the Race Committee, be penalized 20% instead of the traditional 100%, provided the infringement did not threaten the safety of any craft or person; or augment the infringing yacht's speed; or otherwise improve either her position anywhere in the race or her time for completing

the course.

6. If there is doubt as to which Penalty Percent to apply, the more severe penalty shall be chosen.

7. The Penalty Percent for an infringement shall be applied against the number of places obtained by subtracting the infringing yacht's Finishing Place from the place for DSQ (one place worse than the number of "Starters" in that race).

8. In calculating the number of Penalty Places: (a) the minimum penalty shall be one place; (b) decimal parts of places shall be rounded off to the nearest whole number; (c) .5 shall be counted as a full Penalty Place.

9. The resulting whole number is the number of Penalty Places to be added to the infringing yacht's Finishing Place, thus obtaining her Adjusted Finish.

10. A yacht infringing during more than one incident in the same race shall have her most-severe Penalty Percent from each incident totalled (but not exceeding 100%) before calculation of her Penalty Places and Adjusted Finish.

11. When penalties are less than 100%, the assignment of Adjusted Finishes shall not affect the Finishing Places of other yachts. (Thus two yachts may receive the same score in a race when one's Adjusted Finish is the same as another's Finishing Place.)

12. If an infringement occurs between yachts of different fleets, the protest rules and/or penalties of the infringing yacht's fleet shall govern.

An example of the Adjusted-Finish calculation:

In a 20-boat race, the 2nd-place finisher committed an infringement that did not cause the innocent yacht to lose position. When the 20% penalty was applied against the 19 places obtained by subtracting 2nd from 21st (for DSQ), the infringing yacht was scored as if finishing in 6th place. The calculation: 20% of 19 = .2 × 19 = 3.8 = 4 Penalty Places which, when added to 2nd place, gave the infringing yacht an Adjusted Finish of 6th place.

Appendix 4—Limitation of Starters in International Races and Principal National Events

In order to provide good conditions and fair competition, the Permanent Committee of the I.Y.R.U. urges all race committees and sponsoring organizations that are responsible for arranging international races and principal national events to observe one of the following procedures laid down in The Organisation of Principal Events (1973 I.Y.R.U. year book, pages 112-113) regarding the limitation of the number of starters:

(*a*) The number of starters for an international race or principal national event should be limited to thirty boats.

(*b*) Should the number of entries be higher, two cases may occur: either the number in excess is less or more than twenty per cent of the number established above.

Supposing this number to have been established as thirty, if the excess is lower than twenty per cent, a maximum number of thirty-six boats will be allowed to start. If the excess is higher than twenty per cent, competitors will be divided into heats, each heat having approximately the same number of competitors.

(*c*) In the event of a series with an excessive number of entries, the boats assembled will sail elimination races: afterwards a fixed proportion of the best boats ranked will enter the final series (to consist of a minimum of four races), with the scoring to start again at the beginning of the final series.

(*d*) Two examples of elimination series are given for possible guidance, assuming in each case there are ninety entries:

Example (i). The ninety boats are divided into three heats of thirty boats each. Each heat sails the three races without any change in the distribution of the boats. The ten boats best placed in each heat enter the final series, the other boats being eliminated. Scoring in the finals is based solely on the final races, and points for the preliminary races are not taken into consideration.

Example (ii). Obviously, should the entries be ninety, there will be three heats of thirty boats each, should they be fifty, there will be two heats of twenty-five boats each.

Taking the number as ninety, divide the ninety boats in nine groups of ten each lettered A, B, C, D, E, F, G, H, I.

In the first race there will be three heats:—

First heat	A	B	C
Second heat	D	E	F
Third heat	G	H	I

In the second race the heats will be:—

First heat	A	D	G
Second heat	B	E	H
Third heat	C	F	I

In the third race the heats will be:—

First heat	A	E	I
Second heat	C	F	G
Third heat	H	D	B

This does not result in every boat racing against every other boat, but it gets the greatest possible mix. Upon completion of the three elimination races, the thirty boats with the best point scores enter the final races. In case of ties for thirtieth all boats so tied will enter the final races. Those boats not qualifying for the final races will sail in a secondary series.

Appendix 5—Authority and Responsibility of Race Committee and Jury for Rule Enforcement

The authority of the race committee and jury for rule enforcement is well and clearly established in the rules as follows:

Rule 1.1: "All races shall be arranged, conducted and judged by a race committee under the direction of the sponsoring organisation, except as may be provided under rule 1.2."

Rule 1.2: "For a special regatta or series, the sponsoring organisation may provide for a jury or judges to hear and decide protests and to have supervision over the conduct of the races, in which case the race committee shall be subject to the direction of the jury or judges to the extent provided by the sponsoring organisation."

Rule 1.3: "All yachts entered or **racing** shall be subject to the direction and control of the race committee . . ."

Ways and means of exercising enforcement are provided in Part VI, rules 69 to 73 inclusive, which set up procedures for conducting hearings regarding alleged or apparent infringements, for notifying yachts of such charges and for penalizing infringers. In particular is to be noted rule 73 which reads in part:

Rule 73.1(*a*): "A yacht which fails either to **start** or to **finish** may be disqualified without protest or hearing, after the conclusion of the race . . ."

Rule 73.2 "When the race committee:

(*a*) sees an apparent infringement . . .

(*b*) has reasonable grounds for believing that an infringement has resulted in serious damage, or

(*c*) receives a report . . . from a witness . . . not an interested party . . . alleging an infringement,

it may notify such yacht thereof . . . and act thereon . . . as if it had been a protest made by a competitor."

From the quotations and references above, it is clear that the rules provide ample authority to the race committee and jury to enforce the rules and in fact authority beyond that which is ordinarily exercised, while at the same time the rules contain very little which is explicitly directed towards the responsibility which these bodies should assume beyond the deciding of protests. To repeat: "All races shall be judged by a race committee" and "All yachts **racing** shall be subject to the direction and control of the race committee" give the race committee full authority to act on apparent infringements, subject only to the limitations of the procedures established by the rules. It is probably wise that the rules are silent as to the extent to which the race committee is required to initiate proceedings when apparent infringements come to its attention, just as they permit but do not require competitors to lodge protests, but it would seem clear from rule 73.2 that the race committee is expected to initiate proceedings in the exercise of its authority. To what extent should it do so?

It is well accepted that the seriousness of infringements varies greatly, even while recognizing that an infringement, no matter how minor, is still an infringement. An infringement can be so slight that it has no effect whatever on the speed, course or relative position of either yacht; it can be so serious that it results in a collision, disabling both yachts; and it can by almost imperceptible steps be anything between these two extremes. Very few yachtsmen feel inclined to protest a slight infringement that has no bearing whatever on the result of a race. On the other hand, an infringement which involves the risk of serious damage—even if no contact actually occurs—should be, but is not always, protested; nor does the infringing yacht always retire. The same can be said of many other infringements which, while less serious, still result in places gained and lost. It therefore is in the best interests of yacht racing that such infringements should result in the retirement, disqualification or otherwise penalizing of the infringing yacht, and that yachtsmen themselves should be encouraged to see that this occurs.

One way to bring about greater observance of the rules is for race committees to institute more proceedings under rule 73.2. Why has there grown up a tendency on the part of race committees not to do so? There are several reasons. For one thing, the race committee feels that it is the prerogative and therefore, the function of competitors to lodge protests. For another, there is a natural disinclination to increase the burden of holding protest hearings. For still another, it is felt that the race committee sees only a small part of the race and why therefore should it call someone to account for something which happens nearby when there may be many other incidents which it cannot see at all? In some instances, too, it feels that since it is to sit in judgment on a case, it should not also be in the position of a prosecutor. But this overlooks the fact that the race committee is an umpire as well as a judge. When a protest is lodged and a hearing held on an incident not seen by the race committee, it performs a judging function in determining the facts and interpreting the rules to arrive at a decision. But when it sees what it believes to be a clear infringement and no protest results, the rules certainly give it authority and somewhat more than an implied responsibility—assuming the infringement is serious and not trivial, and here of course judgement must be used—to take the prescribed steps of rule enforcement. It is, to be sure, recognized that, unlike other sports in which the umpire calls infringements when and as he sees them, the race committee is required to hold a hearing and give the alleged infringer an opportunity to tell his story, but this difference is a difference in procedure, not in function or responsibility.

The philosophy that in matters of infringements the race committee's function is solely that of judging is sometimes put forward more strongly for the jury, when there is one, than for the race committee itself, but this distinction is not supported by the rules. Rule 1.1 says that "all races shall be conducted and judged by a race committee." Rule 1.2 says the same thing a little differently, in that a jury is appointed "to hear and decide protests and to have supervision over the conduct of the races." Surely the conduct and judging of races includes the right—and the responsibility—to initiate action to enforce the rules. Juries and race committees are expected to be impartial, but partiality is not bringing to a hearing a personal observation of an incident but a desire to favor or penalize one or another competitor. The reason juries are selected for important regattas is not to set up the judging function apart from other functions of the race committee, but to provide as impartial and experienced umpires as possible.

Fully recognizing some of the dangers involved, such as becoming overzealous, race committees and juries should institute hearings under rule 73.2 when there occurs what appears to be a clear-cut and significant rule infringement not protested by a competitor.

Appendix 6—A Prescription to Racing Rule 68.4 Protests Involving Measurement and Rating Certificates

General

A protest under the provisions of Rule 68.4 and involving a certificate issued by NAYRU (IOR or CCA Measurement Rules) should be referred to the NAYRU Offshore Administrative Committee by mailing a copy of the protest and the protested yacht's certificate to the NAYRU

Offshore Executive Director. The Offshore Administrative Committee will make its decision, and may consult with the NAYRU, ORC, or CCA Technical Committees.

Note that Rule 68.4 *requires* the Race Committee to refer such protests to "an authority qualified to decide . . ." and to "be governed by the determination of such authority." The NAYRU Offshore Administrative Committee is the "qualified authority" for questions regarding the IOR or CCA Rules.

The committee of a one-design class which has the responsibility for measurement and the issuing of measurement certificates is the "qualified authority" for questions regarding that class's measurement rules.

Administrative Protests

In addition to the provisions of Rule 68.4, Administrative Protests concerning Measurement Rules administered by NAYRU's Offshore Administrative Committee may be filed directly with the Committee in care of the Offshore Executive Director.

The Administrative Protest procedure has been established to permit protests of rating certificates at any time after issuance, without regard to whether or not the yacht was *racing*.

Any person or organization which has a sufficiently valid interest in a yacht's certificate may use the Administrative Protest procedure, as follows:

1. The protest must be in writing and shall be dated and signed by the protestor.

2. The protest must include a detailed description of the alleged defect(s) and a full statement supporting a valid interest on the part of the protestor such as owner of a yacht holding a rating certificate, a certified measurer, a Race Committee sponsoring offshore racing.

3. The protest must be accompanied by a copy of the certificate being protested and the current address and telephone number of the owner of the protested yacht.

4. The protest must include a statement of the issue the protestor wishes to have resolved, identification of appropriate Measurement Rules, and other appropriate evidence.

5. A copy of the Administrative Protest and supporting materials must be mailed to the owner of the protested

yacht by the protestor.

6. The protest must be accompanied by the Administrative Protest filing fee of $25.

7. The owner of a protested yacht should file a reply with the Offshore Executive Director, in writing, as soon as possible.

8. The Offshore Executive Director will circulate copies of the protest and reply to the members of the Offshore Administrative Committee. The Administrative Committee shall make its decision based on the available evidence and additional evidence it may obtain, and it may order remeasurement of the yacht in whole or part.

9. The Administrative Committee may consult with or refer the matter to the appropriate rule making authority.

10. If the owner of the protested yacht elects to concede the protest or refuses to cooperate in providing for remeasurement, the Executive Director shall invalidate the protested yacht's certificate and so advise all concerned, including the local organization under which the yacht normally races.

11. The decision of the Administrative Committee shall be made as promptly as circumstances permit and shall be communicated in writing to the protestor and protestee.

12. The Administrative Committee shall determine which party will pay and the amount of costs of determining the protest using guidelines as follows:

a) Unless the correct rating of the protested yacht is higher than the protested rating by more than .2 feet of 0.5% (whichever is greater), the protestor will be responsible for the costs. The $25 filing fee will not be counted towards payment of costs.

b) If the correct rating increases by more than .2 feet or 0.5% (whichever is greater), costs will be borne (or shared) by the owner, the measurer(s), or NAYRU, depending upon the determination of responsibility for the defect. The $25 filing fee will be returned to the protestor.

One-design classes may institute a similar procedure with the appropriate class committee or officer taking the place of the Offshore Administrative Committee.

Appendix 7—International Yacht Racing

Union Rules Before NAYRU Prescriptions

8—Recalls

1. Unless otherwise prescribed by the national authority or in the sailing instructions, the race committee may allot a recall number or letter to each yacht, in accordance with rule 3.2(*b*) (viii), using yachts' sail numbers or letters when practicable.

18—Entries

Unless otherwise prescribed by the national authority or by the race committee in either the notice or the sailing instructions, entries shall be made in the following form:—

FORM OF ENTRY

To the Secretary. . . . . Club
   Please enter the yacht. . . . . for
the. . . . . race, on the. . . . .
Her distinguishing flag is. . . . .
her national letters and distinguishing numbers are. . . . .
her rig is. . . . .
the color of her hull is. . . . .
and her rating or class is. . . . .
   I agree to be bound by the racing rules of the I.Y.R.U., by the prescriptions of the national authority under which this race is sailed, by the sailing instructions and by the class rules.
             Name . . . .

             Address . . . .
             Telephone No. . . . .
             Club . . . .
Signed . . . . Date. . . . .
   (Owner or owner's representative)
Entrance fee enclosed

24—Life-Saving Equipment

Unless otherwise prescribed by the national authority or her class rules, every yacht, except one which has sufficient buoyancy to support the crew in case of accident, shall carry adequate life-saving equipment for all persons on board, one item of which shall be ready for immediate use.

25—Sail Numbers, Letters and Emblems

2. Other yachts shall comply with the rules of their national authority or class in regard to the allotment, carrying and size of sail numbers, letters and emblems, which rules should, so far as they may be applicable, conform to the above requirements.

28—Flags

A national authority may prescribe the flag usage which shall be observed by yachts under its jurisdiction.

72—Disqualification After Protest

4. The question of damages arising from an infringement of any of these rules or the sailing instructions shall be governed by the prescriptions, if any, of the national authority.

77—Appeals

1. Unless otherwise prescribed by the national authority which has recognized the sponsoring organization concerned, an appeal against the decision of a race committee shall be governed by rules 77, Appeals, and 78, Particulars to be Supplied in Appeals.

2. Unless otherwise prescribed by the national authority or in the sailing instructions (subject to rule 2(j) or 3.2(b) (xvii), a protest which has been decided by the race committee shall be referred to the national authority solely on a

question of interpretation of these rules, within such period after the receipt of the race committee's decision, as the national authority may decide:—

(*a*) when the race committee, at its own instance, thinks proper to do so, or
(*b*) when any of the parties involved in the protest makes application for such reference.

This reference shall be accompanied by such deposit as the national authority may prescribe, payable by the appellant, to be forfeited to the funds of the national authority in the event of the appeal being dismissed.

3. The national authority shall have power to uphold or reverse the decision of the race committee, and if it is of opinion, from the facts found by the race committee, that a yacht involved in a protest has infringed an applicable rule, it shall disqualify her, irrespective of whether the rule or sailing instruction which led to such disqualification was mentioned in the protest.

4. The decision of the national authority, which shall be final, shall be communicated in writing to all interested parties.

5. (*a*) In the Olympic Regatta and such international regattas as may be specially approved by the I.Y.R.U., the decisions of the jury or judges shall be final.
(*b*) Other international regattas shall be under the jurisdiction of the national authority of the country in which the regatta is held, and if satisfied that a competent international jury has been appointed, it may give consent for the decisions of the jury to be final.

6. An appeal once lodged with the national authority shall not be withdrawn.

78—Particulars to be Supplied in Appeals

1. The reference to the national authority shall be in writ-

ing and shall contain the following particulars, in order, so far as they are applicable:—

(*a*) A copy of the notice of the race and the sailing instructions supplied to the yachts.

(*b*) A copy of the protest, or protests, if any, prepared in accordance with rule 68.3(*d*), and all other written statements which may have been put in by the parties.

(*c*) The observations of the race committee thereon, a full statement of the facts found, its decision and the grounds thereof.

(*d*) An official diagram prepared by the race committee in accordance with the facts found by it, showing:—

(i) The course to the next **mark**, or, if close by, the **mark** itself with the required side;

(ii) the direction and force of the wind;

(iii) the set and strength of the current, if any;

(iv) the depth of water, if relevant; and

(v) the positions and courses of all the yachts involved.

(vi) Where possible, yachts should be shown sailing from the bottom of the diagram towards the top.

(*e*) The grounds of the appeal, to be supplied by either:—

(i) the race committee under rule 77.2(a); or

(ii) the appellant under rule 77.2(b).

(*f*) Observations, if any, upon the appeal by the race committee or any of the parties.

2. The race committee shall notify all parties that an appeal will be lodged and shall invite them to make any observations upon it. Any such observation shall be forwarded with the appeal.

Excerpts from the International Regulations for preventing collisions at sea, 1963 (to be replaced in 1976 by new Regulations)

PART D.—STEERING AND SAILING RULES

Preliminary

1. *In obeying and construing these rules, any action taken should be positive, in ample time and with due regard to the observance of good seamanship.*

2. *Risk of collision can, when circumstances permit, be ascertained by carefully watching the compass bearing of an approaching vessel. If the bearing does not appreciably change, such risk should be deemed to exist.*

4. *Rules 17 to 24 apply only to vessels in sight of one another.*

Rule 17

(a) When two sailing vessels are approaching one another, so as to involve risk of collision, one of them shall keep out of the way of the other as follows:

(i) When each has the wind on a different side, the vessel which has the wind on the port side shall keep out of the way of the other.

(ii) When both have the wind on the same side, the vessel which is to windward shall keep out of the way of the vessel which is to leeward.

(b) For the purposes of this rule the windward side shall be deemed to be the side opposite to that on which the mainsail is carried or, in the case of a square-rigged vessel, the side opposite to that on which the largest fore-and-aft sail is carried.

Rule 20

(a) When a power-driven vessel and a sailing vessel are proceeding in such directions as to involve risk of collision, except as provided for in rules 24 and 26, the power-driven vessel shall keep out of the way of the sailing vessel.

(b) This rule shall not give to a sailing vessel the right to hamper, in a narrow channel, the safe passage of a power-driven vessel which can navigate only inside such channel.

Rule 22

Every vessel which is directed by these rules to keep out of the way of another vessel shall, so far as possible, take positive early action to comply with this obligation, and shall, if the circumstances of the case admit, avoid crossing ahead of the other.

Rule 24

(a) Notwithstanding anything contained in these rules, every vessel overtaking any other shall keep out of the way of the overtaken vessel.

(b) Every vessel coming up with another vessel from any direction more than 22-1/2° (2 points) abaft her beam, i.e., in such a position, with reference to the vessel which she is overtaking, that at night she would be unable to see either of that vessel's sidelights, shall be deemed to be an overtaking vessel; and no subsequent alteration of the bearing between the two vessels shall make the overtaking vessel a crossing vessel within the meaning of these rules, or relieve her of the duty of keeping clear of the overtaken vessel until she is finally past and clear.

(c) If the overtaking vessel cannot determine with certainty whether she is forward of or abaft this direction from the other vessel, she shall assume that she is an overtaking vessel and keep out of the way.

Rule 26

All vessels not engaged in fishing, except vessels to which the provisions of rule 4 apply, shall, when under way, keep out of the way of vessels engaged in fishing.

The International Rules apply to vessels on the high seas. The Inland Rules apply to vessels on inland waters including coastal areas.

Copies of the complete regulations, both International and Inland, may be obtained from the United States Coast Guard.

MARBLEHEAD RACING ASSOCIATION
1973 SAILING INSTRUCTIONS

(A good example of the form a club's sailing instructions should take)

All Races Sailed Under Current Rules of N.A.Y.R.U. Adopted **April** 1, 1973 except as modified by these instructions.

Official notices of the MRA are posted at the pierhead bulletin boards of the Boston, Corinthian, and Eastern Yacht Clubs.

ELIGIBILITY

Marblehead Racing Association events are open to any yacht upon completion of the proper entry form and payment of applicable fee. Yacht owners in submitting entries to the MRA agree that whenever their yachts participate in any race sponsored by any Marblehead yacht club, whether sailed by the owner or anyone else, they shall have aboard in good usable condition, all safety equipment required by these instructions.

SCORING

Scoring for each of the three MRA series and for the MRA season's championship will be as follows, unless a class elects to score differently, in which case an officer of that class must submit a properly documented system to the MRA for approval by May 6.

Scoring for each MRA series will be based on the four best results of each yacht, except that all disqualifications shall be scored.

Season's championships will be computed on the total score of the three series.

The low point system will be used in all classes. The winner is scored 3/4 point, second yacht, 2 points, etc. A yacht withdrawing or not finishing is scored 1 more point than the number of yachts starting; a yacht not starting is scored 2 more points than the number starting. A disqualified yacht is scored 3 more points than the number starting.

Cancelled or abandoned races which are not rescheduled will be scored as fleet byes.

All scheduled races prior to receipt of entry will be scored DSQ.

PRIZES

MRA season championship prizes for first and second place will be awarded to each class. Prizes for subsequent places will be awarded based on the number of entries, i.e., 11 or more, third place; 20 or more, fourth place; 30 or more, fifth place.

Duplicate prizes will be awarded for tie scores.

The MRA will award first place prizes to each class for each of the three series within the season. The Boston, Corinthian and Eastern Yacht Clubs will award first place prizes to each class for each day's event, provided six or more properly entered yachts compete. Such prizes must be claimed at the desk of the sponsoring club by the evening of the race.

STARTING

● All lines will be between a white flag on the committee boat and a mark of the course or special mark. The outside line will generally start at the outer circle of marks; the middle line in the area northeast of Cat Island, and the inside line in the area west of Cat Island.

● In the event of postponement after previous classes have started, the first gun will become the preparatory signal for the next class to start.

● Yachts starting prematurely will be hailed by sail number when possible. The recall shape will be used, in addition to an audible signal.

● In the event of a general recall, the class recalled will start five minutes after all other classes on its line have started.

● The start of each class will be indicated by hoisting a red shape, in addition to an audible signal. The shape will be lowered 30 seconds before the next class is to start.

OUTSIDE LINE	MIDDLE LINE	INSIDE LINE
1:30 Warning (White Shape)	1:00 Warning (White Shape)	1:30 Warning (White Shape)
1:35 Preparatory (Blue Shape)	1:05 Preparatory (Blue Shape)	1:35 Preparatory (Blue Shape)
1:40 Etchells 22	1:10 Tempest	1:40 Rhodes 19
1:45 International One Design	1:15 5-0-5	1:45 Day Sailer-Blue
1:50 U.S. One Design	1:20 110	1:50 Day Sailer-White
1:55 Shields	1:25 Lightning	1:55 Town
2:00 Soling	1:30 420	2:00 Preparatory (Blue Shape)
2:05 210	2:15 Warning (White Shape)	2:05 Corinthian
2:10 Ensign	2:20 Preparatory (Blue Shape)	2:10 Bullseye
	2:25 Tempest	2:15 Herreshoff 12½
	2:30 5-0-5	2:20 Widgeon
	2:35 110	
	2:40 Lightning	
	2:45 420	

● All yachts must keep clear of the starting area until their preparatory signal, or risk disqualification.

MRA COURSE PATTERNS

△	USUAL COMMITTEE BOAT STARTING POSITION	▲	USUAL COMMITTEE BOAT FINISHING POSITION	◭	USUAL COMMITTEE BOAT STARTING & FINISHING POSITION

MARK DESCRIPTONS

Mark	Description	Mark	Description
1.	Not used	21.	Marblehead Harbor buoy 2 MH
2.	Racing Mark 4070 yards, 143 deg from Marblehead Light	22.	Racing Mark 1400 yards, 010 deg from Marblehead Light
3.	Racing Mark 2975 yards, 127 deg from Marblehead Light	23.	Marblehead Channel Lighted buoy 3 (Chappel Ledge)
4.	Racing Mark 3900 yards, 118 deg from Marblehead Light	24.	Marblehead Channel Lighted buoy 4 (Mid-Channel Rock)
5.	Racing Mark 4900 yards, 119 deg from Marblehead Light	25.	Cat Island Channel buoy 5 (Martin's Rock)
6.	Racing Mark 5750 yards, 124 deg from Marblehead Light	26.	Racing Mark 2400 yards, 090 deg from Marblehead Light
7.	Racing Mark 6400 yards, 132 deg from Marblehead Light	27.	Racing Mark 3200 yards, 089 deg from Marblehead Light
8.	Racing Mark 6670 yards, 140 deg from Marblehead Light	28.	Racing Mark 3900 yards, 080 deg from Marblehead Light
9.	Racing Mark 6600 yards, 150 deg from Marblehead Light	29.	Eagle Island Channel Buoy 5 (Pope's Head)
10.	Racing Mark 6100 yards, 158 deg from Marblehead Light	30.	Eagle Island Channel Buoy 4 (Rising States Ledge)
11.	Racing Mark 5300 yards, 165 deg from Marblehead Light	31.	Eagle Island Channel Buoy 6 (Cutthroat Shoal)
12.	Racing Mark 4300 yards, 168 deg from Marblehead Light	32.	Marblehead Channel Buoy 6 (Eagle Bar)
13.	Red and Black Gong at Tinker's Ledge	33.	Marblehead Channel Buoy 5 (Coney Ledge)
14.	Racing Mark 2700 yards, 147 deg from Marblehead Light	34.	Marblehead Channel Buoy 8
15.	Red and Black Can at Volunteer Rock	35.	Salem Channel Lighted Bell Buoy 9 (Power's Rock)
16.	Racing Mark 2200 yards, 139 deg from Marblehead Light	36.	Cat Island Channel Buoy 4
17.	Racing Mark 2500 yards, 118 deg from Marblehead Light	37.	Cat Island Channel Buoy 2
18.	Marblehead Red and Black Bell buoy	38.	Whistle Buoy 1 at Newcomb Ledge
19.	Marblehead Harbor buoy 1 MH (Gordon Rock)	39.	White and Orange Bell Buoy "DG"
20.	Marblehead Channel buoy 2 (Archer Rock)	40.	Bell Buoy 4 at Pigs Rocks Outer Breakers

COURSE INSTRUCTIONS

he course posting board consists of two vertical columns. The forward column designates the course pattern by letter, as illus-ated herein, and the approximate magnetic compass bearing to the first mark. The aft column designates the marks to be unded, reading from top to bottom.

he course shall be sailed leaving all marks to port when the course pattern letter is posted at the top of the forward column, ove the magnetic bearing. The course shall be sailed leaving all marks to starboard when the course pattern letter is posted at e bottom of the forward column, below the magnetic bearing.

he starting and finishing marks must be honored only when posted.

hen the mark for a second or subsequent windward leg is changes, a committee boat at the leeward mark will display code flags U, the number of the new mark, and its approximate compass bearing. Two audible signals will be sounded for the first yacht each class reaching the leeward mark, and a single audible signal will be sounded for each other yacht.

n all courses yachts must pass to the east of Tom Moore's Rock, Tinker's Island and Roaring Bull and shall not pass between at Island and the rock south of the island. Middle line competitors shall not pass between Eagle Island and Mark 32.

ourses may be set up to three (3) minutes before any start.

he time limit shall be 6 PM for each class, unless changed verbally after displaying code flag L, prior to a blue preparatory shape. he Course may be shortened at any posted mark after the start.

MARBLEHEAD RACING ASSOCIATION CHAMPIONSHIP SERIES SCHEDULE

Date	Event	Sponsor	High Tide-EDST
Monday, May 28	First Series	Boston Yacht Club	8:42 PM
Saturday, June 2	"	Eastern Yacht Club	12:52 PM
Saturday, June 9	"	Corinthian Yacht Club	7:26 PM
Saturday, June 16	"	Boston Yacht Club	12:35 PM
Saturday, June 23	"	Eastern Yacht Club	5:33 PM
Saturday, June 30	Second Series	Corinthian Yacht Club	11:42 AM
Wednesday, July 4	"	Boston Yacht Club	3:15 PM
Saturday, July 7	"	Corinthian Yacht Club	5:56 PM
Saturday, July 14	"	Boston Yacht Club	11:33 AM
Saturday, July 21	"	Eastern Yacht Club	4:10 PM
Saturday, August 4	Third Series	Eastern Yacht Club	4:26 PM
Saturday, August 11	"	Corinthian Yacht Club	10:21 AM
Saturday, August 18	"	Eastern Yacht Club	2:56 PM
Saturday, August 25	"	Boston Yacht Club	9:16 AM
Saturday, September 1	"	Corinthian Yacht Club	3:01 PM

SAFETY EQUIPMENT

• All yachts must have the following safety equipment aboard at all times, in good working condition, subject to in-ction by a Race Committee or U.S. Coast Guard Auxiliary vessel: (1) Coast Guard approved life preserver or buoyant vest each person aboard (buoyant cushions and ring buoys not acceptable); (2) compass, box or wrist style permissible; foghorn or whistle, powered by hand, mouth or power; (4) adequate tow line; (5) adequate bailing device. In addition, h yacht must carry a copy of the current sailing instructions. Light displacement boats must be able to swamp without king. The MRA strongly recommends each yacht carry adequate anchor and line.

• **Failure to comply with these requirements constitutes grounds for disqualification for the remainder of the season.**

GENERAL INSTRUCTIONS

• **Yachts must report withdrawal or disablement by showing sail number to the Race Committee until acknowledged number, or by reporting in person or by phone to the club sponsoring the race immediately upon coming ashore. YC–631-3100; CYC–631-0005; EYC–631-1400) Yachts not so reporting will be disqualified.**

• Postponement or cancellation signals will be flown from the yard arm of the yacht clubs before the warning gun.

• In case of fog, in addition to sounding the committee boat's bell, the following horn signals will be given when on tion: outside line – single blast; middle line – two blasts; inside line – three blasts.

• A yacht should be prepared to identify by class and sail number the yacht immediately ahead and astern of it upon quest by the Race Committee.

• The first division of a class sailing in two divisions must display a blue triangular marking at the peak of the mainsail least eight inches on the hoist.

PROTESTS

• Any yacht having cause to protest must promptly display Code Flag B in the main rigging and keep such flag flying til acknowledged by the Race Committee. Protests must be filed in writing at the sponsoring club within two hours of the ne the protesting yacht finishes the race. Protests will be heard at 7:30 PM on Monday.